THE TEMPLE OF ZEAL

Chronicle 27

Panagiota Makaronis

KREA PREA (TM) Est. 2012

Copyright © November 2025 Panagiota Makaronis

All rights reserved

The characters and events portrayed in this book are fictitious. Any similarity to real persons, living or dead, is coincidental and not intended by the author.

No part of this book may be reproduced, or stored in a retrieval system, or transmitted in any form or by any means, electronic, mechanical, photocopying, recording, or otherwise, without express written permission of the publisher.

ISBN: 978-1-7641457-8-7

Cover design by: Copilot
Written in; Australia Victoria Melbourne Craigieburn.
Publisher; KREA PREA (TM). Est. 2012

I dedicate The Temple of Zeal Chronicle 27, to those who had entered my realm & Disturbed my Peace.

For they needed a feast; I had no time for them & instead of letting me go;

There ego took over, & the decision to rampage my head, summon me with an offering of drama, trauma, & a failed attempt to replace a trace, that had me aggravated; by the attempt.

An entrance to a scripture & a chapter unwelcome. You caused so many negative effects; just to get my attention. In the end what can I say; all it did was make me dislike you & you disguise the truth. Just to skip another foolish event.

Time to set it alight, hit back & face that disturbance head on. All so I can get back on track & feed off the impact.

Patience is a Virtue! Allowing Love & Hate Amalgamate will bring forth War to Peace. It will go to such distance; it will reshape a connection; not worth the troubles.

Handing me a failed Redemption here on end, will bring forth War to Peace to the individual who harmed my peace.

Amen

The trauma that we face, is a trace; created by man. Forced by a Demon, generated by an unforeseen source.

Where the third eye, becomes bare; free from despair. Forced by those who have left an ancestral stain to your domain. It is part of a trace that will hand you a clue.

A given opportunity to rise beyond scrutiny. Then to return for repetition, based on a yearning. To cleanse clear and break that fear.

Trap that trend & release the Demonic energy; back to the sender freestyle. No need to cut a chord or piece together that feast.

Because the test was part of a request. Made when you were building that foundation waiting for it to settle. where the wall will only collapse when you relapse.

Where every approach will hand them a debt. An impression that will Delete, Delay & put the corrupt through hell all the way!

Amen

PANAGIOTA MAKARONIS

CONTENTS

Title Page
Copyright
Dedication
Epigraph
INTRODUCTION 1
CHAPTER 1 5
CHAPTER 2 15
CHAPTER 3 28
CHAPTER 4 41
CHAPTER 5 54
CHAPTER 6 67
CHAPTER 7 80
CHAPTER 8 93
CHAPTER 9 106
CHAPTER 10 119
About The Author 135
The Theatrical Melodia of my Life: Chronicle One 141

INTRODUCTION

The Temple of Zeal Chronicle 27; is a renewal, to ground me from an old wound. My attention to detail brought redemption. I could sense my reality changing, from recovery into deception. Returning to hit back with passion; burnt out. Releasing the demon; as I pause an effect.

Leaving me once again stagnant to my development. I was pushing through trying to fight off; one to many evil spirits. Whether dead or alive it did not matter; they were Demonic. They were soul searching feeding off the trace; it had me replace them. For I did not want a part of their world.

They tried every way possible to enter my realm; a scheme to break my theme. The lie was overpowering me. If I did not give in, the destruction; would be worse than the interaction. My truth had me overwhelmed and the lie overzealous. Distracting my existence with perseverance.

Waiting for me to return so they can get another crack at it. An attempt to break my spirit, heave at me at every tremor; once again second guessing. Just so they can cover up another misdemeanour. For those who were conspiring to get in, were attempting to sabotage me from within.

Summoning me with a lie, assuming that will cover up the truth. In fact, it led me astray, pushing me forward. It was lining me up for one more chance to break the silence in advance. I had to repeat another trace at the end of that case. Handing me the key I need to cancel the corrupts method.

I once again ready and willing to succeed with intention. never aim to take my power, break my cycle, or devour. An assumption part of that everlasting trace; an ending to that race. A dishonourable effect left me haunted. A past, living in the present trying my luck; to break the chain.

My patience, was tested, trapping me in the corner. Leaving me facing a lead to a presentation where the corrupt had the power to breed. All so I never rise above that trace; facing another case. A slow but steady motion, that became a picture-perfect moment; ended their mission.

It served me a component to that proposition. It led the corrupt towards a pathway of heresy. For what was to come to fruition, became my way of accepting; failure along the way. Because Several were hidden under the raider. It had me waiting to return, break the chain and start again.

For my wheel of fortune; once again left me sturdy. Ready to break that trace, ease my pain and start again. It took me in and had me trending from within. It was overwritten with aggression. Not only I was forced to remain silent; but I was torn in more than one direction.

I had to find solace in a task, that had no sense of

reality. Those who knew were working in unison with those who had a clue; under scrutiny, trying to get through. Only to witness the drama unfold, and the trace remains to be seen; not silent in between. A work in process; testing their existence.

Not only it was over powering my scripture. I knew it was done on a deliverance stance. Just to lead me astray, fast forward to another damn day. A gamble for me to press replay, where my morals were being tampered. I could sense my reality being torn in ways; more than I can handle.

The only way to remain sane was to give in and play the game. It had me live a lie step into a bribe and wait for it all unfold; I was put in the lime light purely to give the corrupt a chance to relight a flame. One that had burnt out many moons ago. The reason behind it was to show up and show off.

It created a piece, that had fed off the outcome, it had me share a piece. With he, whom wanted to repeat. Then take the initiative and press delete. Please that beast and overcome another feast. My passion was intensified with the notion. That the corrupt had me forced, to hit back with remorse.

Devoted with caution, was part of a cause of action. A trace that will hand me an abreaction. A task achieved, well served, and reprieved. It served me well, presenting me with a key; that led me through hell. An astonished event, that lined me up, for a wish a trace; that had me dish it out.

Handing those who knew a favourable attempt to hit me too. It was part of a burning desire to relight a flame. Where this time around, what I knew, had me on a common ground. Where I stand tall, in the realm of society; trapped no more. For my social light lit only in the limelight.

It was part of a compelling event; led towards a direction to vent. Because I had been fighting a lost cause just to remain grounded. The only trace and treasure to repeat had me measured. It was the one thing that had me start fresh. A final feast at the end of that trend that saw me heave.

I was to release and follow up on a feast. It was part of a vendetta to release that dilemma. Just to find Peace in between the lie the Cheating and the final meeting. An expectation that served me well at every destination. Haunting me as I hit redemption. An Enlightenment to the next destination.

AMEN

CHAPTER 1

❖ ❖ ❖

WHAT A BLUNDER

When you speak your mind and steal the corrupts thunder. On the edge of reason, entering a method concocted by the corrupts second trial. It gave me a chance to hit back in advance. It was part of my safety net, to lead the unjust towards a journey; they cannot adjust to.

I was on the edge, trapped once again, in the middle of a chaotic event. It had me face a trace, leading the corrupt towards a pathway of travesty. Lessoning the load, was one way of accepting a challenge. The other had me abused and left me facing the accused.

Wording it to he who created the trace, just to find myself in a disposition. Had me releasing another proposition to the opposition. It was part of a final restoration, that had me facing an allegation to that investigation. For I was given a reason to return and hit back with treason.

For those who entered, were trying their luck too. It gave me a second chance to get back on track and advance to the next trace. Handing the corrupt a dead end at the end of the race. I was left to repeat return and press delete. Delaying the corrupts method handing them a test; to release peace.

I was led on, lied to, wasting no time, because I knew; that lie will get me through. Now that I am here I could not careless. All I could do to resist that persistence was unravel and repeat another trace to that case that caused an effect. It had me travel towards one thought to the next.

It gave me a trend that had me face a dead end. Where each trace had me repeat, replace give in and force me to break the cycle from within and begin a new inning. Where I get in and witness the corrupts hint of madness. A challenge that served me a well it gave me a second chance.

A challenge that will help me fast forward to the next level. Skipping a trace trapping those who condition the mission and phase that competition. It was part of a valid response. All so I can catch up and feed off the energy that had me face another dead end at the end of that trend.

I had to beat the corrupt to the punch, trap them in the middle of a feast. Because I wrote that riddle, it handed me a spiral a spindle effect. A passion to belt them to the ground and raise the buck. For their destiny was prewritten, while I was on the mission of making it happen.

For that reason, I was forced to repeat, hit back and press delete. Because I had the freedom to report, rebel against those who fought against my will. I lost my way forced to press replay, left to delve into a method that had me feed off the trace. That served me well at the end of the race.

I was left to trade in, trace that win; follow up on a new beginning. The loss took me in and urged me to face that space, that was giving me impression I never lost that trend. What I gained was the freedom to break the system; for that is what broke my vision in the end of that competition.

Because my hope was creating a feast, it led me towards a journey; with no inner peace. Where the only thing left was the trend, that had me interacting with he who knew. For he who knew was creating a war in my peace. I never release, explode; losing my ignition to my intuition.

There was no trend, the hope to my dream ended in-between. For he who had a clue was on my raider; entering my realm unwelcome. Trying to break my spirit so I never catch-up, pitch in nor ever win, an inning. I was too busy fighting a lost cause, breaking the system; feeding off the admiration.

It had me serving he who saw me easy, it was creating a war in my mission; so, I lose my intuition. Handing me an interaction to break every section; handing me the wrong selection. For I was given a chance to hit back in advance. For that conscious awareness took me on a path that led me astray.

It had me state a fact and force my way in, about to repeat and follow up on a new beginning. It was part of a trace, a given reason to respond to the corrupts final case. It had me hit the corrupt back with treason. Because I hit a dead end, the corrupt lost the will and the faith to hit back.

It had me face another curse, at the end of that verse. I was taught a lesson, returned for a trend. It led the corrupt towards a journey where their mission was destitute and their poison was evoked. It had me face another trace, get in, and feed off the trend that had me follow up on a new tread.

It was part of a case that served me a trace. I was given a reason to accomplish a goal and present the corrupt with a verse to hammer them in the head in the end. Where I get in and heave at every accomplishment. That is when I knew I hit a review. For I thought it was the last resort.

I was heading for a fall; it trapped me and gave me a failed attempt. The corrupt were warning me to lose that trace hand them the case and feed off the tremor.

It served me well at every dilemma. I was on the mend waiting to be taught a lesson in the end.

I had to release that beast that saw me as an easy target. I was taught a lesson a given, and a reason to hit back with treason. So, when I reached the end, I no longer had to rush a thing; because I was already in. Trying my best, to let the corrupt in, witness a threat a debt and a dead end in the end.

It was part of a trace that made me sense that the test will cave in on the concept. It had me step in me and undo a new review. A reason to break the system and feed off the trend that had me failing. Falling in dispute and dire straits in the end of that final dividend.

I had to follow up on a review. Head towards a destruction that forced the corrupt to follow up on a past mission. All so I can engage in an entrance to the unknown. It had me facing the corrupt and feeding off the injustice. It had me force to hit back with remorse.

I had to trace and feed off the trend that had me follow up on a threat in the end. Because I was on the move the ending that was, I was pending had me cleansed. It was part of a never ending pay a gamble that led me astray. I had to come to terms with the fact the corrupt had come first.

It broke the silence, and raised an alarm. I was on the move facing a trace, it had me leading the corrupt to a destination that will hand them a desirable phase. It was giving me the power embrace the truth accept defeat and follow up on another trend in the end of that forthcoming blend.

Emerging with the trace, that made me fail at the end of the race. I lost all momentum because the key that was handed to me was part of a reality kick that had me face another final degree. For the trap became a second trial, where I was living in denial, trying to catch up face another fact.

I had to feed off the corrupts challenge, give in to the road I was on. Protect my spirit from falling into the wrong hands and breaking me in advance. The path I was on ran its cause; I had no reason to repeat a treason. The only thing left was to trap get in, and break the silence from within.

It was part of a test that had me progress. It gave me the energy to feed off the corrupts confession. Handing them failure at every diversion. It was to break the silence and face a trace. All so I can claim my division, breaking the opposition. Remained on the edge trapped in the middle of a trend.

Warning me the only case left, was the one the corrupt concocted in the end. I had to feed off the trend, that forced me to get in and repeat another inning. I was warned of the outcome, but not left to repeat it. So, I decided to delay it, so when the time come, I could replay it.

It had me face a trace, step into the old and feed off the trend. It brought me forward in the end. I could not relate to anyone. I hit an ending, that was pending; concluding the obvious. I was taught a lesson, led to believe, the worst just to hand the corrupt a chance to curse a rehearsal.

With every verse, I was given a curse, with every trace I was handed a case. It gave me the trend to hit back and face another dead end. So, when I hit the end the only failed attempt will be the one the corrupt served me. So, when I fell it forced the corrupt to hit back; facing a test to that quest.

It gave me a final request, laughed at me at the end of that test. It had me requesting a new conquest, a challenge that took me in and fed off me from within. It was part of a trend that led me to believe the only thing that forced me in; was that one thing that had me facing another win.

Even then the hit, the run, and the obligation to face a competition was invalid. It was part of a trace that gave me a trend to hit the corrupt with a dead-end. It had me change a trend; on the edge. It forced me to hit back with revenge. It faced me with a failing attempt a conspiracy to pay off a debt.

For the corrupts method, was part of a dead end. It was passed, with a curse, that had me pending to come first. For the corrupt were pretending and I was stepping into the unknown unwilling. It had me hit back feeding off the trace that pushed me off track.

The power of suggestion was no longer in the mission. It handed me a redemption, killing the corrupts method; at every forceful momentum. It was part of a never-ending battle. It gave me a second chance to hit back in advance. Breaking the cycle creating a piece that had me face a feast.

I had to reverse a curse, cause an effect, and take that trend to the next level. It hit me with a dead end. I had to refine and follow on a journey that took me in; with a brand-new reflection. I was on edge of reason, where the conclusion to their vibe was part of a fake and false tribe.

For all I knew, there was no case to review. The conditions were based on predictions. It was part of a past endeavour, that had me warned' I hit the corrupt with a vendetta. Where this time around I stood clear, causing an effect reaching my pinnacle. Creating a defect to that corrupts final release.

I had to rise to the occasion. Prepare myself for another investigation. It caused an effect and left me rummaging for the truth. All while the rest were waiting for me to fail; so, they can exhale. It was the only way for me to return, and feed off that trend that had me warned once again.

I was releasing that demon, that had relaying messages. It was creating a threat and hitting the corrupt; just before I hit an encore. For all I knew I was on the move trapped in the middle of a lie to get the truth. I gave in locked the corrupt out, continued on my journey; no longer living in doubt.

The condition was part of the mission; it was the lie that got me by. No longer will it help the corrupt finalise that trend. I returned with the same key, purely to break the corrupts cycle feed off the remainder of that curse. It was the beginning of a trace that had me evaluating the case.

For what it was worth the troubles were stirred. For he who used method to harm me, thought it was a game. It had me return and rehearse for a verse. It was servicing a key, that led me to a final degree. Where I get up, force my way in, feeding off the challenges; that had me face a new trace.

I was on the move, waiting for the last cast to come through. So, when I reached my peak the end result will face a trace. It will give me the entrance, that I need to break the silence and succeed. Giving me the impression I was hit with the device to that contradiction; with added admiration.

I was led to believe that every dream was no stronger than the lead. For the drama took over the theme; it became a failed scheme in between. Served well, while I tear the corrupt apart, giving me a second chance to feed off the drama. Creating a trace that will serve me well at the end of that spell.

It gave me a trace, that had me face a case. It was part of a given, to hand the corrupt a chance to break the cycle. It forced me to repeat, restore my energy and press delete. All by delaying every focus, forcing that trend that had me repeat a dead end. A case, adding to that troubled ending.

It caused an effect and rebelled against those who assume the edge of reason caused an effect and handed me a defect. Just because they created a commune, where the energy that forced its way in had focused handing me the input to face another trace. Preparing me for one more case.

I was served well at the end of that trend. Because I was pushed in the corner waiting for the trace to overcome another case. It gave me a second chance to eradicate. Force my way in feed off the concept create a deception in the corrupts direction. The return, will turn to my favour.

Not only they will return, with the same scheme but the theme will change. Turning against each other. A raw deal that will be part of a steal, where the skill will hand me the thrill of the chase. It will give me the power and the energy to release erase and find peace after the fact.

Feeding off the journey that had me claim my true worth. Was the start of a new thought the one I needed to feed off the last resort. For that feast that brought out the beast, it became my way of accepting defeat. For I was living in a trend that had me fall into a dead-end.

CHAPTER 2

◆ ◆ ◆

WHY MY DESTINY TOOK A TURN

I took a wrong turn towards the right direction. I fought off my perpetrators with a curse; they cannot reverse. I had them questioning their method, and their motivation. I had them feeding off my transformation, purely to catch them in the act and present them with a fake and final trap.

A manifestation to that destination; had me reaching my potential. I passed that test requested a new trace, took the old with the new and replaced it with a curse I could reverse. All I had to do was undo another upcoming review. It was leaving the corrupt destitute, fighting double time to survive.

I found myself in a position rising above the incantation. It had me reaching the next level sooner. Just so I can enter, feeding off the adventure. It had me facing another road towards recovery. I found my limit; creating a challenge that served me well; when I hit the upcoming spell.

My presentation was validated I was taught a lesson. Left to withdrawal, just to catch up from that failed attempt. It that gave the corrupt a chance to return and belt me in advance. I responded with a final feast. Trapped in the middle of a trail an error and final dilemma; trying to release peace.

By the time I reached my target I was released. For he who knew, led me to face another trend at the end of the race. I was about to face another trace, giving me the intention I was about to fall into another redemption. I needed to get back on track replace the case; before I continued.

For that course of action, was paused. It had me face another trace, giving me the power to catch up and face another race. Warning me there was no given presentation, just a trial an error and a final investigation. I gave in, just to feed off the trace that presented me with a final case.

The corrupt, took their time, for they were cheating. They were stringing me along handing me nothing but false hope to claim their truth; just to keep them strong. Where I gave in trapped in the middle while taking a challenge, it had me feed off the trend; break the silence and start again.

Leading me to believe that their method will keep them balanced. It had me face another trace; create an ending I could relate too, all while I feed off the concept. All so I can get in and win another trial. Where in the end of that trace I was certain; I hit an ongoing disgrace.

I had to give in, and boost that energy that had me feeding off the synergy. I had to get over that win, that had me listed. For every trace was part of a case, based on a past dilemma. It had me delayed handing me a tremor. It was part of a challenge that had me on the no how.

I was on the edge, no reason to erase that presentation. Because it became a mind reading game, an energy that had me embrace every trace. There was a boundary, that was not met and I was put in a position that had me wrong all along. Led towards a journey that created a war in my peace.

I swore black and blue that every faith I had landed into; will pause effects. Handing me the evaluation to return for an investigation. I was stuck reaching my potential and even then, I was pushed in the corner hitting a dead-end. handing me the pleasure to return and feed off the trend.

It had me reach a point of no return. It was all part of a list of affairs that lined me up for failure. In fact, it took me in a saved me; handing the corrupt a final review. A challenge where they lose hope and never get through. Because I gave in on them long ago; I found serenity in that valid test.

It gave me an early rise, a trial an error; a desirable dilemma. It put me in a challenge that served me a role. It forced me to repeat and fade away in silence. All while the rest compete compel and attempt to reach out to me assuming I had the final review to feed off the anomaly.

I was torn, given a reason to follow up on a treason. As I reached my pinnacle, the statement of a fact, will hand me the trend that will put me back on track. Creating a defensive mechanism that will serve me a road and push me off the edge; hunting down those who created a war in my peace.

A thorough trail, and a trip down a mile; where the memory will hand me denial. Giving me the impression that every damn solution was based on the corrupts resolution. For the trend will hand me an allegation to release that beast that forced me off the edge.

I had been trapped for a while; I had nowhere to go and nowhere to turn. The conclusion was to release stand to find peace. Not give in and allow the corrupt to return and deny me access at the end of that final. Where my light was dimmed and my journey was trapped.

Where the end result was conditioned by the corrupts final mission. I left stranded, taught a lesson, and led to believe the lie was part of a trace. It had the corrupt breed another final feed. All so I can catch up and feed off the corrupt. It was handing them the deception that created that resurrection.

Preventing the corrupt from ever returning; for a revelation. It was part of a feast, where every case will serve me well and hand me peace. I was served wrong, and put me through hell. Just so those who knew can get crack of creating a war in my peace; all so they can steal another feast.

For the corrupt were to feed, prepare me for a new improved journey. I was off with a challenge that had me break the system entirely. It had me retrieve, feed off the concept, and break the silence all while the energy that faced me to hit with a periodic effect; a challenge that will serve me well.

Praise the corrupt no longer, because this time around; what goes around definitely, comes around. Those who created the war in my peace, were about to get a trend not worth denying. Deleting or delaying in the end will bring forth a challenge that will harm the corrupt existence out of the force.

Because the journey was free, the trace was a key. I was left to break the system entirely. They were caught red handed, facing me as if they had no fear. All because they assumed they were encouraging me in a fight; I will take the bait. In fact, it created a war in their vicinity.

It brought me forward; put me back on track. I was to return for a scheme, creating a theme in between. Just so I can get a glance of what I thought will bring me forward. Destroy that test that had me in control so I never progress. Shame a defensive game; tricking he who tried to trick me.

While they attempted to clear a debt, I was on the other end left to repent. I had to retrieve, what I thought was the last resort. Hitting back, had them giving in, that is when I knew they were trying their luck to face me and hit me with Bad Luck. It was part of a choice to have the corrupt rejoice.

A dark secret that become part of an unprecedented event, made me see I hit a final degree. It took me on a journey that had me face another trend. All so the corrupt can return and vent, hitting me with a curse you can reverse and finalise that test that had me retrace that unique debt.

It gave me second chance, to relive a dream; witnessing I hit a nightmare in-between. It was part of a challenge that will serve the corrupt well. Handing me the validation and the intermission that gave me a grand entrance to the next competition. I was about to come first finalising that curse.

It had me getting up to mischief so, I can undo what I did, without wanting too. I helped the corrupt get through preparing them for another clue. So, when I hit the end the only thing that had me face another win. was the trace that handed me the troubles to erase that forthcoming case.

I was left to repeat, giving the corrupt a rundown. For the outcome to end in my favour, I had to repeat replay and press delete. Just to hand the corrupt a chance to return and break that cycle that had me face another trace at the end of the race. I had to get in and test the corrupts patience.

For the edge of reason had me face another treason. I had to follow up on a journey that had me wonder what did I do to deserve such a blunder. I felt trapped in a chaotic situation. For the corrupt took me in had me had me feed off the trace; that forced me to embrace; the end of that case.

I had to press delete, so the corrupt can catch up. Follow through to the next overview. Causing an effect, was breaking the silence. It was taking it to the next level without losing, a thing. It had me face a new inning. Forced to repair a troubled outcome, trapped in the middle of a second trial.

Those turn of events, led me to stand clear. All so the corrupt can continue to follow up on a rise. I was wording it my way, wondering off; every step of the way. For a while the corrupt were playing a role that stirred the pot. I was stuck hitting a dead end, failing every trace that served me well.

Where I hit a hold up, and created a piece. It forced me off the edge straight into a kind heart. Just to see justice come to be at the end of the race. Because I was stalling and took it all in, I had to repeat repair and try my luck handing the corrupt bad luck. It had me on the edge; above and beyond.

I was ready to pledge, just to catch up and face another trace. The next test, became part of my development. It gave me a second chance to hit back in advance. I had to process that confession and accept what was done. For the outcome was part of a trend; that served me well in the end.

So, when the time come, I had to return to break the silence; hitting back with a vengeance. It had me face another trace trick he who had me forced to hit back remorse. So, when they hit me ran, I was provided with energy forced to recover. Hand the corrupt a dead end at the end of that trend.

The decision to revise and follow up on a scheme, had me redeem; break the silence in-between. For what the outcome would be, will hand me the resolution to break the silence. It was to face another trace that had me refrain; from returning and belting the corrupt again.

Because I caught them in the act of attempting to write my destiny. It served me well and presented me with a curse that had me reverse and come first. It was facing me with a reality that had me overcome scrutiny. I was hit at every direction, facing another manifestation.

A constant reminder I hit the end of that supervision and handed the corrupt superstition. This time around I took over my destiny. Never shall I feel betrayed by society's values. Never shall I be attacked by those who return for a theme to make me a victim to their scheme in-between.

For that trace was based on a case that never fell through. It had me borderline about to lose that one thing that forced me off the edge. Straight into a dead end that had me face another trend. It had me waiting to break the silence and repeat another trace; at the end of the case.

It was causing an effect repeating a debt. It had me catching up with the curse, then returning for one more verse. It took me back to what I thought was part of a case. It had me replace a trend at the end of that test. It forced me to silently to return for one more chance; to hit back in advance.

I took another chance to hit back in advance. It faced me with another territorial event, that had me break the silence and repeat after the fact. A path that created the piece had me release and follow up on another factual event. it took me in and forced me to undo that review that was finalised.

It made no sense to me, how far the corrupt took it. All I knew it gave me the power to return and devour. Dividing and conquering every trace that come my way. It faced me with a trauma that had me forced to hit back with remorse. For a trail of thoughts that were not true took over my rise.

It left behind what I thought will give me the power to override another slide. I was hit back with a case that served me well at the end of the race. I was on the other end, facing a new trend. Making sure the end of that road ends in my favour. Leaving the corrupt suffering in slavery.

Warning me I hit a right to cut the corrupt in two. The only thing left was the trace that had me face and uncover up another condition to that mission. It led me towards a presentation that forced me embrace that everlasting emotional discharge. A memory that left me holding on to the past.

It was creating a piece, enforcing the corrupt to own up. It had me facing another trend at the end causing an effect and presenting the corrupt with a curse they cannot reverse. Because I had to return rehearse and come first. Feeding off that trend that served me well in the end.

Even though I felt low, with nowhere to turn. A trail of burden left behind gave me the energy to feed off that synergy. All so I lose that trace and never face another final case. For he who knew, warned he who had a clue; to face me and fail me right through.

As if their power in numbers and friendships; handed them freedom. Ther trace became part of a game it was based on a case that hit me at the end of the race. I had to claim another game and gamble that method that had me remain vigilant all the same. A method; pushing me into the deep.

A soil, that was dark and mirky, drowning in filth. I was lit on fire, drenched in oil; burnt to a crisp. Then forced to rise above the coal, the ash and remain still wanting to love the same. In hindsight the loneliness and darkness I felt, when I was going through hell was a lesson lived and learnt.

It led to believe that I deserved that burn. It gave the corrupt a chance to unite with whom ever to make my life not worth living. Every time I got through to the next level the challenge became over powering and I hit an ending that was pending; leaving me second guessing.

All I did was give in, feed off the trace, and face another case. Fading in the distance was part of a trend that had me repeat and replace that threat in the end. I was not handling things well, handing it back to the sender threefold. Was my way of letting go and presenting the corrupt with a test.

It was the only way to catch up, and feed off the trace and face another case. It had me keeping up with the program, praising he who knew and he who had a clue and every trace I entered had become an adventure that served me well and had me on the edge surrendering every key.

It had me finalising my vision and preparing me for a point taken and a trace forsaken. It was handing me a competition that served me well at every disposal. All while I was on the mend, surrendering that key, that forced me off the bend. It had me sitting in admin, faking it all.

For that false and final taste, handed me a test that had me erase a request. I was given a reason to step into a melody of affairs. It had me erase, that trace that forced me to compete, compel, and face another ongoing spell. It had me make excuses just to prolong the obvious.

I had no trace to erase, just a final case, on my own to roam to the next final frontier. A challenge that will bring me forth, and help me face another terrible faith. It had me lose that control that fed off me whole. For that reality kick was based on what I thought was the last resort.

I was on the move, locked in, trying to get out. Catch up and finalise that test that had me progress. Warning me the only thing left was the energy that faced me; when I hit the end of that dynasty. Only to witness my patience ran thin and I realized the corrupt were on the move trying to get in.

When they caught up, I was faced with a hint of madness. So, I never reach my high standards. The decision to let go and set it all free, trapped me as I took it all in and fed of the disadvantage from within. It had me on the edge ready to break the silence and feed off the trace.

I was thrown a bone, left to chew on it waiting to be called up. Only to see I fell for the lie the cheating and the corrupts final meeting; that had me face another day. It had me forced to repeat and hit back with remorse. That is when I knew the only thing left was let go and face the facts.

There was no trace no trend no freedom to pretend. It had me on the case ready and willing to hit back with a final uproar. A skill that will feed off the trace and face me with a case it had fed off an ending that was pending a challenge that had me case another trace at the end of the race.

I hit another final hunt down where I get in and feed

off the trace that faced me at the end of the race. In reality I was taken for a fool, was wasting valuable time on a journey handing me the evaluation to claim a new destination. I was handed was a lie to get me by.

In the end the only thing that had me face a new beginning, was the one thing that forced me to repeat the same game again. It served me well and presented with a coil of affairs to put the corrupt through. Just to release that final infatuation; to that manifestation.

CHAPTER 3

◆ ◆ ◆

RETURNING TO FEED OFF THE CORRUPTS DIGNITY

The journey had me reach my peak; warning me. I was stepping into the unknown with each stepping stone. Where ever I turned, there was always a kind heart, trying its hardest to harvest. It had me on the run, waiting for the curse to reverse. A return to that turn; handing me a key.

It was forcing the corrupt to repeat, then rebel against one another. Just so I can get a glimpse of a future endeavour. The vendetta took its toll; I was stuck hitting back with a curse; I can reverse. All I had to do was come first and even then, I had to rehearse and follow up on a feast.

Every time they found me fit, I was served a challenge that had me seize. It was a trend that had me enforce a cause of action; feeding off the abreaction. I had to return for one more chance to press delete. The only thing that had me get in, was the journey that served me well from within.

I was to hit a home run and create an outcome that will serve me well. I was entering the unknown presented me with an upcoming spell. All while I continue to sail through, and try not to look back. For the trace had me evaluate another trend in the end. It was handing me the present forecast.

I needed to portray a new outlook; and step into a trace; that had me face another case. So, when I got in, I had caused an effect. It gave me a second chance to pretend and protect myself from that threat. For every step I took there was a challenge that had me face another case.

I was given the opportunity to rise above that scrutiny. I was handed the wrong end of the stick. Everything that was to go wrong went wrong. I was pushed of my limits, left to suffer in silence. All so he who caused the fault; can hold the forte. Control my destiny and feed off me whole.

It a created the war in my peace; then return and blame me for that feast. For each day was to get better, in fact every trace had a case. Every given opportunity was handed to me with the conscious awareness. I had the freedom and the foundation to return and break the cycle at every arrival.

I weas handed the energy, added with theory; to revive another dive. For every follow up, gave me the reason to return and hit back with treason. The vision to that notion come first and the corrupts method come last. Handing me the opportunity, to release that beast; that brought me forward.

I was on the move, hitting the wrong, making sure they do not remain strong. I get in feeding off the trace that took over the case. It was forcing me to repeat and face a final endeavour. Feeding off the corrupts method and breaking the silence that took me in. Forced to face another bad taste.

I had to remain silent, create a piece feed off the concept; with a kick-off. All while I hit back, and follow up on another feast. I was to rebel against, those who enter my realm; feeding off the trend s when the time come start again. It had me back up and watch it backfire in the end.

All while I continue to roam and undo a review. I had to report give in, remind myself there was no time to follow-up on a test. For the old, had started, a new venture and I was stuck feeding off the trace that had me overrun another outcome. It created new avenue, that forced me to review.

In the end of that trend. I was handed an exposure to the corrupts final method. Where the only way out was the way in and even then, I had to embrace that energy that had me face another siren at the end of that presentation. It had me failing the next destination with a reservation.

I had to overcome the loss from that outcome. I was meant to gain wisdom all the same. Warning me the only thing left was the energy that had me process another program. I had to refine that force that hit me back with remorse. Just to begin anew inning; it was part of a thought program.

A challenge that created the piece; had me request another feast. It served me a purpose, preparing me for a test, haunting those who return for one more request. It taught me a lesson left me to embrace, it forced me to replace a case. Just to prove that my innocence; was being tampered with.

It will help me overcome another validation to that outcome. I had to beat it all to the punch; and finalise that hunch. Returning to feed what I thought was starved. It gave me a chance to hit back in advance, overlooking that theme that brought me a test the next request.

So, when I reach my pinnacle, I could return and face the music. For he who tried to join to me was a mistake. It faced me with an informal win. It had me trapped in the middle of a riddle it took me in, and repeated it. Having me relive a feast, to that piece that forced me to overcome an outcome.

I had undo and overcome an event that was not meant

for me. I was stuck trying to please he who was harming me. Just so I can catch up and feed off the debt that had me overpower undo and devour another threat. It forced me to rehearse a theme and reverse the curse back to the sender.

For the corrupt were way off; on the edge. Straight into a doom's day full of regret. It had me step into the unknown, a road that served me whole lot of dreams it gave me a second chance to step into the unknown facing a trace to that case that caused an effect.

It presented me with a verse I could rehearse. It was giving me the impression I was about to be taught a lesson. It left me to repeat that final deception. It reserved me the right to outdo and disclaim a review. It forced me to release, create a feast; a test to restore my energy once more.

It faced me with a trace just before I was hit with an encore. I was to move forward and release that beast; that had me outraged. On the edge returning for a yearning. It gave me a chance to return for one more glance. So, when I reach that peak the information given; had me at peace.

It caused the effect, and slowly come to be; handing me unity. They were to provide me with a truce, and hand me a clue periodically. I was to power up give in; break the silence from within. It had me on the edge with a spiral effect. Providing me with a challenge at request; a free ride to prevail.

Preventing the corrupt from sailing by, it had me face

the truth. I was taught a lesson; I had to revive feed off the challenge that had me survive. I was held up, that restored me at every expense. It had me hold on to the forte, that brought me back; feeding of the task that put me back on track.

I hit a hold up, that gave me the power to undo and devour. It helped me overcome an outcome; that will serve me well in the long run. I was taught a lesson lived and learnt; a valuable one. A second chance to undo get back on track. Feed off the trauma; forced to hit back with a vendetta.

I was on the move presented with a curse I can reverse. All I had to do was release the beast, the rest were to follow and I was to find peace. It had me finalise that feast that forced me to overcome and rely on the corrupts method so I can get by. Hitting he who knew and he who had a clue.

Warning he who knew, and he who had a clue, there was no chance in hell to; return for a what. It had provided the corrupt with a brand-new review. There was a challenge, that had me on the edge waiting patiently for the corrupt to pledge. All while I catch up face a trace at the end of that case.

I had to follow up on a new improved journey, face the facts, and feed off the tact. Then when the time come, grace my presence with Glory. For space become part of a case that took me in and followed up on another win. An outcome where I get in and feed off the second trial from with.

I had to case every trace, face every forum, create a trend that will serve me well. So, when I reach my pinnacle, I could redo and follow up on another clue. Just so I can catch up and create a trend that will serve me well in the end. Every thought will force me to hit back with the last resort.

I was taught a lesson creating a trace that will force me to repair a trend in the end. Where I get in catch up face the corrupt with a challenge; where they lose their identity. All while they follow up on a key that will serve me well. Preparing me for an upcoming catastrophe.

I hit the end, face a trend, and create a final vendetta. All so I can catch up and feed off tremor. It was over before it begun. I had no choice but to decline and break the corrupts silence. It had me hitting back with a curse I can reverse. I was to declare innocent and take a dive to the other side.

Greed got the best of two worlds and neither of them got in. I was forced through challenging he who knew and he who was supposed to hand me a clue. It had me delayed and facing a final review. I took it all in and hit the finals; a trophy to that dilemma that had me hit the end of that tremor.

For he was about to be screwed, took a turn for the worst and I come first. All so I can get through first and last and face a fact. All while I take the initiative and feed off that tact. It was a test based on a past request. Just to follow up on a feast, face a trace at the end of that lease.

It had me on request, where I had to free myself from a

test that had me follow up on a pause and effect. While I gain wisdom and trap those who outdo and override a clue. For I took the time out and fed off the doubt. Trapped he who forced me to get in. All while repent; feeding off the attempt.

For I was on the other side, personally being attacked by he who was informed. He was haunted by the past, living in the present. Hounding me so he can continue to relive another deception to that redemption. He served me well took that trend and fed off the evil eye; I gave him in the end.

What a test I had to revive, just so the corrupt can reside on the other side. Complimenting me so I can overdo another review, had me in an awkward position. Forced to repeat and rebel against those who knew. I had no response, when I caught up. That is when I knew I hit he who had a clue.

Serving he a loss and I a gain, had me repeating the same game. I had to undo follow up on another review, feed off the concept so I can skip the corrupt right through. I was seen as an easy target, forced to repeat replace and follow up on another challenge at the end.

It was part of a get rich quick scheme; that went belly up. The corrupt had no chance of retrieving what they stole. The journey was taken; and I was forsaken. That is when I knew they were screwed   I come out the other end burnt; ready to rise above the shame; that was handed to me all the same.

I was feeding off the trace, that served me well in

the end of the race. I was to get in, cause an effect release that beast and force my way through. All while I condition the mission handing the corrupt a dead-end at the end of that competition. I had to trace that key, that had me forced to hit back.

It was part of a game that served me well all the same. I was given reason to sweeten the deal; it led me towards a validation that had me informed. I hit a presentation the lined me up for an investigation. It was part of a raw deal that had me face another ordeal.

It gave me the energy I needed to declare my soul for the taking. I took it all in it had me following up on a truth; while I press dare. Because I knew the corrupt were returning for a yearning. The thought of giving in had handed me the evaluation to return and hit back with a final manifestation.

For the method was mistaken; by the forsaken. I had to reach my pinnacle stir the pot raise the buck and overcome another outcome. For each test had me enclosed with another foreclosure. I was hit with a contest that had me on demand. Feeding off the energy that had me progress.

All while the rest process that interest at request. I was Isolated by the truth, because of the past abuse. For every trace that took me in, had impersonated my truth. All so I can claim a division to the game. Every trace served me an alliance, handed a confirmation that faced me at every violation.

It was to bring forth a reservation, to that resilient

cause of action. It was handing me the urge to force my way in. It had me feed off the new improved journey from within. I was to bring forth peace after the fact. Then when the time come overcome that outcome.

I was taken for a fool I took it all in and gambled my truth. I was given the opportunity to return and feed off the scorn. For all I knew, the journey was a challenge. It was part of a trace to reserve the right to accomplish an everlasting feast that had me on the edge fighting for my life.

It was part of a case where the condition had me contradiction the mission at every disposal to that mission became part of a competition. Not only I was given a reason to hit back with treason but the follow up to the next test; gave me the reason to hit back with treason.

A thought that had me rise above and beyond. It gave me a second chance to repeat and repent all while I got back on track and fed off the debt. I was served me well and in the end of that threat there was a test that had me on the edge trapped in the middle of that threat.

Where every legendary status, stated a fact. It had me sitting in the back burner finalising that threat. Handing me the energy to create a trace that will break the corrupts silence at the end of the race. It was part of a trace that hand me the edge. It had me forced to hit back and remain silent.

All while I continue to hit back, a trend at the end of

that free ride; become solid. I had to return to reclaim another division to that competition; it had me on the edge. It had me rising above and beyond a brand-new tread. I had to follow up on a scheme that had me standing pretty.

It took me on a journey beyond my abilities; because I sold my soul to a dynamic demonic spirit. It took me on a journey that forced me off my limit. I had to step forward not back, create a piece just to get back on track. It had me on the mend trying my hardest to blend; while the others Harvest.

It forced me to reminisce, look forward not back; take a moment to get back on track. For he who followed me to end of the road, took it all for granted; faced me with a trend that forced me to pretend. Then decided when I was on the move forward cause an effect and feed off the defect.

It had me follow-through to the next vile avenue. It led me towards the end of that road; faced with a curse I can reverse. It was part of a challenge that had me come first. It had me hitting a rehearsal to that forthcoming curse. Every time I was forced to decline; the corrupt had opened a new case.

It had me on the edge, facing another trace; at the end of the race. I was left to revive and create a challenge that taught me a lesson. I was taken for a ride and given an opportunity to repeat, what I thought was part of the last resort. Even though the trend ended with a no show.

I still managed to complete the task, without needing to deal with the loss. For the gain put me through a challenge that had me face another damn bad day. It was then I knew I was faced with a final review, and the only thing that stood before me; was the one thing that had me face a trace.

It gave me a final frontier; it forced me to hit back. Even when I could not see the road clearly. I was still given an opportunity to finalise that momentum that handed me the freedom; At the end of the race. Forced to give in, replace, and follow up on the heat of moment.

It gave me the momentum I needed to retrieve. Because I had to follow up on a new improved key, a trace that served me well brought me forward; all while I was going through hell. That is when I knew I was forced to obey a certain rule, a given reason; to give the corrupt a chance to repeat.

Meanwhile I remain vigilant to a game, that had me gamble my truth away. I was on a path, that was not for me, it was to drive me absolutely insane; while I lose my integrity. Just to give the corrupt a chance to remain the same. Certain that the game they created had integrity.

In fact, there was no truth, it was a lie to push me in the corner so I never get by. Leaving me ambushed, warned to outdo that outlet. Because I was left outdated and inundated with so much information. The only way for me to register was let go and leave it all behind.

Because the task, was an impossible case to embrace. I was not interested in the case, I had nowhere to go, no place in my heart to let go. So, when I reached the end of that task, the only thing left to begin with; was the trend that brought me forward. Trapped me from within.

It became a non-win situation on both ends. The energy that created the piece had no freedom. The foundation was wrong; it was not strong enough to release. The only thing left, was begin a new task and create a new piece. Follow up on a feast, take the initiative; challenging the corrupts method.

CHAPTER 4

◆ ◆ ◆

A HAUNTED TASK THAT ENDED IN FREEDOM

Because there was no end in sight, the conclusion was clear as day; I was being brainwashed. The corrupt saw me as an easy target and led me on; purely for them to remain strong. I was forced to repeat, hit back and press delete. All while the corrupt were determined to return; finalise outcome.

I was left to return with the same old game, an age repetitive competition. Leaving me warned I hit at admission leading the corrupt to another competition. I was stepping into the unknown, forcing the corrupt to fight back and feed off the impact. A disposition that handed me a proposition.

A disposal that served me well at every arrival. It drove me towards another mission losing a competition. I had repeated the last resort. It presented me with a faith that had me return with the same old game. A vision that handed me a deterring composition against the opposition.

It forced me off the edge straight into a violent attack. A vague stagnant affair, that caused havoc to corrupts second trial. For he who knew wanted to repeat a challenge. Then hand me a chance to cause an effect. I was back on track serving me a test, and a trace to help me face a threat.

I had to resurrect from that threat that had me on the edge. It pushed me forward just to case close another threat. It was part of an image that was hitting me with a feast. It served me a restoration from that trace that warned me I was on the wrong side. Hitting an ending to that was manifesting.

It was pointless affair that had me facing another trace to that case. A presentation that was never to come to fruition. It led me towards a journey that served me well. I was given a reason to replace the old, start new and feed off the concept that had me on review; facing another point of view.

I felt trapped by he who knew, left to return, and overlook a view to roam with an overview. It was part of a journey that was pending for a while. It took me in and fed off me from within. Leaving me struggling, on the road towards a second trial. A method that warned me I was left to silently evolve.

Meanwhile the rest solved the issue, that lined me up with a dark thought. Giving me the impression that I was handed an intervention. In fact, I was introduced to a kind heart, then without notice left to stir the pot with a rotten thought. I was turned; several on my raider trying to return.

I had to release that beast that left me to repeat another feast. I was to cause an effect, return with a defect. When I reach that everlasting response the end result; will no longer carry a burden. Hitting the end was raiding my head; holding me to contempt. My way of getting through without delay.

I watched a dream collapse and shatter, no warning whatsoever. It turned my life upside-down, I had nowhere to go, nowhere to turn, my light shown but I could not find that inner peace. I had so much pride, I lost the energy to survive. My instincts kicked in so did my anger.

I was so fed up with the road I was on; I could not find a balance or remain strong. I hit a hold up, fell into the deep, the mind was forcing me to undo a clue. It did not matter how far I took it, as long as I forced my way in. The only drama that took me in was the one that had me feed off the outcome.

An addiction to kick a fuss was kicking me right before I hit an encore. It had me release, find peace and force the corrupt to repeat rebel and feed off the trace that put me through hell. It gave me a second chance to hit back in advance and follow up on a review.

It forced me to redo, repeat and follow up on an assessment. It had me on the move, restoring my energy and repeating a new improved journey. It gave me a second chance to repeat and rebel against the honest truth. The corrupt were hiding that test; that had me forced to digress.

In the end there was a trend; that served me well. It gave me a second chance to put the corrupt through hell. That is when I knew I was not leading the pact; I was heading to a path I could review. A fall that will help me come through. I had no freedom nor foundation to reap.

What I had was a key to press delete, and follow up on a faith, less likely to eradicate. It forced me to erase a case and follow up on a key to serve me well while I put the corrupt through hell. For the trace had me erase another case. A curse I can reverse and a challenge to help me come first.

Where the only thing left was a given, a challenge that had me reach my peak. It handed me the information I need to refine and follow upon another time. A trace that served me a case had me return for one more turn. I was taught a lesson, forced to hit back for no reason.

I reach my peak, and an entrance to that path will hand me a method so I can come last. I was given a chance to hit back in advance. Restoring my energy, all so I can get in and feed off the trace that had me face a curse from within. It was part of a task that had me face an end repeating a dead end.

I had reached the end of my tither, wrapped up in a position worse than the mission. I had to return and face another trace, a given reason to hit back and face another case. I hit my pinnacle, just in the nick of time. I was forced to return and top it off with a trend; that had me pretend.

I was hitting the end; in fact, it was the beginning of a new trend; a trace I can replace. All I had to do was return and acclaim a final review. I was hit with a curse; I can reverse and a challenge that had me face the truth. It was part of the reason, that gave me the energy to hit back with a follow up.

I had no reason to rebuild, because I had faced the trace that brought back memories. I was hit back with a case then when I least expect it return for one more key to replace the old the new and the energy that had me face another review. A challenge that had me return and feed off the ongoing.

For that trend that brought me forward in the end, was based on a case. It led me to believe that the energy that took me in had me face another violation to that manifestation. It was part of a new case that caused and effect. The trace became valid; I had no reason to return and hit another ballot.

The end of that road was based on a trace that had me repeat and replace. I hit a pinnacle and I had to get back on track finalising the end of that path that forced me to erase a case. I was faced with a follow upon another case. I hit back with a trend that had me forced to rebel against the odds.

I was on the mend ready to break the cycle in the end. Then without fail refrain from losing a game. I had to follow up on acle remain sane while the rest were kicking a fuss. In the end I was heading for a beheading. Where the only way out was release that beast; it forced me to undo that review.

Just so they can get ahead and I fail a division to a game that was gambling my truth away. It had me facing my destiny, without the knowledge I needed to get through. I had to skip a challenge escape a chase feed off the truth break the silence and continue on my journey.

As if the chase had no meaning, and the trend that had me start again. It was a threat that had me face another trace. I was given a reason to hit back with a feast. It was part of a trace that had me face another case. It took me through to the next final review. on the path of creating a cheap shot.

A challenge that had me face another trace; was part of a trend that served me well in the end. I was given a trial, an error, and a faith to delete delay and feed off the tremor. It gave me the option to catch up and face a case. Cancelling he who knew and he who had a clue.

I had to face what I thought was last resort it gave me an entrance. I had to follow up on what I thought was the last service, before I entered that path way that had me questioning the corrupts method all the way. Where the interest to that feast had me face another test on request.

I had to develop a trend at the end of that tunnel. It was holding me back; it had me face another case just to condition the mission and feed off that proposal that saw me easy target. It gave me the power to undo and finalize that review that had me face another case; at the end of the race.

I had to free myself from a journey that pushed me off track. So, when I reached my peak, I could review and overload; while I reveal another skill. The one thing that had me raid the heads of those who took me in graded me before I had a chance to face another case.

For I was taken for granted by those who were on the path of creating a piece; just to get ahead. I was feeding off the corrupt, so I can continue on the road to slaughter that drama that fed off me like no other. Warning me what ever come my way, had been destroyed by the corrupts overlay.

I was nowhere near the road; that led me astray. I had to position the mission, feed off the competition. Then when the time come, follow up on a trace that was extended. Where I saw the world hit rock bottom. I felt the loss the trace the trend and the final feast; come to an end.

Just before I had a chance to hit back in advance. My thoughts took over; I fell into the deep; forcing my soul to face another goal. For what it was worth, the energy that come forth had me on the edge supporting a new challenge a task that served me well at the end of that forthcoming spell.

A trial took over and the error, pushed forward another trace at the end of the case. It was based on the corrupts final dilemma; handing them terror. Where every thread caused an effect, it brought me forward and help me resurrect. For everything that come my way, had me face another bad day.

A forethought in the end of that trend will break the cycle. It will end the race sooner, handing me a violation that served me a method. It had me facing another trend. Causing me to praise that trace that failed me at the end of that day. It gave me the passion to release another diversion.

A manifestation from a past trace had come to fruition. I hit the end of that motivation forced to break the corrupts final destination. Stepping into a deep and meaningful reservation. It had restored an energy that had me face a case. Force me to hit back at the end of the race.

It led the corrupt towards a path; that had me hit back with a risk. I was taught a lesson left to break the silence feed off the trend that had me hit a dead end. It was part of petty threat that had me case close every trace that saved me at the end of the race. Warning me the end was not clear.

The safety net, I was led to believe I was in took me in. On journey that was troubling me from within. It led me towards a pathway that had me face another fear.

It was part of a trend that hit a dead end. It caused an effect and broke me, when I hit the finals and made it until the end.

I was stuck in the middle of healing from a fall that broke my wing. Trying to get back on track was no way to live. I was constantly rejected, trying to come to terms with the fact the troubles that had me face a trend led me towards a pathway that had me face another trace in the end.

I rose to high, to fast, several participants on the other end; waiting for me to fail. Just so they can progress and sail. I had to rebuild on a new me, where this time around accepting the fact, I had flaws and the trace that had me face another case. It was my way of getting back on track.

I was on the edge stuck feeding off the impact; cancelling that method once again. Just to get a glimpse of a future case a crack at a final feast where every thought took me on a journey that had me hit the last resort. For the corrupts method had me on the go casting a spell.

It gave me the impression I was restoring another competition. Just so I can pledge trace another case and keep up with the program while I get in and replace another trace. It had me face another pain that took me on a journey where I to pass and heal once again.

An anxiety that had me face another trace, giving me the power to outdo and devour. It had brought me back to where I was, before I fell for that encore. It was part of a curse I had to reverse just to finalise that road to recovery. A passion that brought me forward took me on a journey.

Where I found my freedom to revive and follow up on another dive. I was meant to be given a reason to hit back with treason. A follow up on a journey that led me towards a trial an error and a final dilemma. For I was on the move, trapped in the middle of a chaotic event.

A challenge that handed me the trial had me revive a tribe. A warning that hit me when I hit the end of that dive. It forced my way in and feed of the trace; where do I begin. before I was hit with unity it ended in travesty; one cycle at a time. It was the beginning of a new trial a trace that took me in.

It was the start of something magical; I was stuck in the past living in turmoil. I just could not see the positive side of that unity. On my raider for a while, I was given a reason to hit back with a trial. It was part of a follow up on the condition I return, reap a reward, and face another trace.

I was reporting those who knew, feeding off those who had a clue. A follow up on a past case facing another trial an error and a final feast. I get in and release that beast that made me face a feast. before I was hit with a challenge to beat. I was given a momentum, to catch up and face the truth.

For the debt had me on the edge of a threat. A final treat, just before I was pushed towards an encore. A challenge that had me wasting away, what I thought was important at the time but in fact it was me fighting off the inevitable a challenge that had me see; I hit a final catastrophe.

Where I got to the end, I felt cornered nowhere to turn no freedom to pretend. No foundation to outdo just a final review. Facing what I thought was the last resort. For whatever come my way there was always a trace that will hand me the drama to repeat and restore my energy once more.

For that dream ended in tragedy and I gave in. Handing me the energy to follow up on another window of opportunity. For what I thought will hand me the outcome, had me face another trace to an ending that was pending. It had become a challenge with no outcome just I surrendering.

It had me face the worst, encouraged by the curse. I got in facing another win, I was taking my time. Waiting for the right moment to stand my ground. I just could not deal with another drama. I had to face a trend that led me to believe that the worst had hit me with a curse.

I hit a dead-end and the only thing left was the trace to begin, a new inning. It was part of a traumatic event that had me face a new inning. Now I was stuck in the middle of a past endeavour a fear that took over my present. Stuck, fighting those demons that had me face another tremor.

The foundation was harmed, the freedom to return was scarred. For that allegation was a mistake to begin with. I was torn in more than one direction, where the corrupt played it purely to have me fail another resurrection. It took me in, failing me from within. Holding on to that one more inning.

I lost hope when the trace had me entrapped, in the middle of a case. I was given a reason to respond to that respite; on the hope I return for one more fight. For the passion to repeat another vision was part of the corrupts competition. An impression that had me face that final pace.

A destination to that manifestation became part of an interval. It had me on the move second guessing everything. I could not fight another trace, from within. It created a nightmare in-between. I was stuck in a time warp waiting for the trace to erase that test that had me confess.

For that trend in the end, became part of a final dead end. It handed me a test that served me a trial and error and a final dilemma. For I was given a chance to save my soul and feed off the energy that fed off me whole. Before I hit the end of that trace, it had me on the edge, privileged.

Preventing the corrupt from ever returning for a yearning. It served me a purpose and trapped me while I was trying to fight off a dead end. All while I get in freely press replay; and terrorise the corrupts method all the way, it had me face another fear.

Waiting patiently for the next game to come to fruition. Warning me once again, I hit a final a presentation that handed me denial. So, when I reached my pinnacle, I could create a piece force my way in and release that beast. It took me on a journey that created a trial an error.

It had me come forward hitting a final dilemma from within. I had to repeat, push the corrupt forward with a final denial. Warned, I had caused the wrong effects, it took me on a journey that had me face another trace. I was taken in and failed a trace from within.

CHAPTER 5

◆ ◆ ◆

WHEN THE CORRUPT PLAN AHEAD

Time to follow up on a new treat, release that beast that forced me to repeat. It had me open a door and replace the old with the new all so I can skip that too. I had to place an order face another final feed off the concept so when I reach my limit the door is no longer ajar.

Stating a fact creating a piece was my way of releasing peace. An attempt to get back on track, was not wrong, it took me on a presentation that had me face an informal investigation. It gave me a chance to face my fear. Follow up on a new improve clue, trap that skit; skip the corrupts method.

The corrupt were no longer welcome. I was on the move trying to mend another dead end. Where I was given a reason to accomplish a competition. It had me on the mission trying to face a case. With the troubles that had left me facing another way out. It presented me with a curse I can reverse.

A challenge I could rehearse, had me come first and face another trace. For all I had to do was undo and follow up on another overview. A trend that was pending, had me surviving on a what I thought was part of the game. For it was pointless affair that had me facing a dead end in the end.

For every mission had a composition. It led me towards a journey that had me break the mission. I was on the other end, waiting patiently to be called up. Little did I know I was taught a lesson by the corrupt, so I never get in or face another inning. I had to regain conscious awareness again.

When I reach my peak I start again, assuming everything that had me face an ending had me rearrange everything. I had inkling that the corrupt were trying their luck. I hit another inning warning me I was on the edge, trapped in the middle of a new beginning.

I was starved of affection once again. I had to define and lead the pact and then release that demon that had me back on track. A challenge that made me see the trend in the end; come to be. All so I can get back on track and face a chaotic event. Within; investigating a trial an error a final vendetta.

All so I can catch up and feed off that trace, that pushed me out of place. For all I wanted to do was push them off track. Where in the end of that trend I had to repeat what I thought was the end of that mission a start with a better ending. I was given the premonition to hit back with a new vision.

I was given a promotion where I needed to feed off the premonition. Where I was given a reason to hit back with treason. It took me on a path that had me facing another restoration to that manifestation. It had me case closing a past event; taught a lesson and left to vent.

It had me face a trace feed off the mission from within. I was back, creating a better piece, forced to undo and release that beast. Where in the end, the only test that had me progress, was the one that hit me at the end of that feast. It forced me to redo and accomplish another goal.

I was up to no good, because I hit a dead end. A journey that was for keeps; there was no return no loss or exchange. A challenge that protected me at all cost, gave me a chance to hit back in advance, where the end result will further. Handing me key to finalise an ending that was trending.

It faced me with an error added with a tremor that forced the corrupt to pretend. It gave me the passion to erase that case. Causing an effect and feeding off the injustice, that served me well and broke that spell.

In fact, I was given a reason to return; presenting the unjust with a rough ending.

In the meantime; bribe them with a curse as I reverse that verse. With a challenge that forced me to replace a trace. Then press replay, because I was given a reason to hit back with treason. There was a place in my heart, that had me repeat; a final destination to that manifestation.

For what it was worth I was handed a clue, served a presentation, and skipped that too. It had me hitting a reservation. All so I can rehearse another verse to that curse. It was part of a trend that handed me the evaluation, that took me in. It broke the silence from within.

A service that had face a reality check was true. It had me finalise another point of view. For every time I was led on, I was warned that the trace had me overcome another case. It had me presented me with a pause an effect; giving me the power to resurrect.

I searched for an end that was trending. A warning I was taught a lesson. It forced me to repeat facing another trace. It had me finalising that method to claim another division to a game that had me run free. A new congregation, handed me a foundation that had me reach another destination.

Where I took it all in, feeding of the trend that warned me from within. I was on the move facing another fear. Leading the corrupt to destination, that took me in; faced me with fear from within. Because I was entering the unknown I had to delve into a final review; facing another avenue.

I had to face a failed attempt, catch up, and prevent the corrupt from returning for a yearning. All while I give in to the corrupts administered event. It had me face a test to that threat. It warned me I was about to hit a dead end. Waiting for the corrupt to return for a free ride.

They were asking for trouble and the only thing that will hand me the win was the trace that forced me to erase the one thing that brought me forward. It was part of a trend that left it to the imagination. It was a threat that gave me the power to resurrect.

It handed me the energy where the corrupt had a restoration to that manifestation. Handing them a loss to that gave me the free ride where they lose their position and their recognition. Where the power to return for a chance to administer that test; had them failing so they never progress.

Handing them taste of their own filth. Was my way of creating a trace and a trend that had me face another dead-end. I was on the edge waiting for the corrupt to pledge. They were on my raider winning another threat to that debt. It had me curse a verse so I can reverse.

My peak had come and I made a difference I n the end. I was taken in with a new trace that had me face a case. It had me hit back and face another trial an error and a final dilemma. A challenge that haunted me back then cursed me. It gave me a second chance to follow up on a review.

It had me undo and create an overview of affairs. I was chasing he who knew and feeding off he who had a clue. Presenting me with a demonstration, that had appeared to be facing another internal investigation. A challenge I could endure. It was part of a validation to promote energy.

It fed off me and put me through hell, because the trend had me refrain and start again. A warning that come to be, had me face another reality. It served me injustice, and unprecedented event. It had me face another trace. A faith that become uplifting, an served me entertainment in the end.

It forced me to review, facing a tremor. It broke the system right through, hounding those who knew to stand their ground. Giving me the opportunity to hit back with a curse. I was to be served wonders at the end of that verse. Not given a challenge to help the corrupt come first.

Cursing he who knew and follow up on a theme to scheme too, just to give forth a step into that wrong review. I was taken for a fool for that invasion that served me peace had me face another feast. I was in between the road to recovery and the path to deception.

A validation to harm the corrupt at every destination. Became my piece, a challenge that will help me rise and look beyond that enterprise. It had me face a fear, all while the rest attempt to break that cycle. Forced me to return with an arrival. It had me feed of the test so I fail.

I was to look from within, look no further; face another

test, just to progress. For I was to resurrect and feed off the energy that brought me a prediction that handed me an evolution. For I was given a challenge that served me a trace that had me on A constant battle of fighting off the drama.

I was on the run, harmonizing every trace. A given trend, so I can break the cycle and start again. I had to defeat the corrupts method. Where each test created a feast, where the corrupt had to confess and finalise that tradition that handed me a proposition. For in the end, I had no request.

All I had was an interest, to restore my energy feed off the presentation. Wake from the dead towards an awakening. That is when I knew I had no foundation or the freedom to undo another review. It was part of a resurrection to follow up on another manifestation.

In the end, all I had to show up cause an effect and start a new trace. I was given a threat to repeat and rebel against the corrupts final spell. I had to come to terms with the invasion prepare the corrupt with another manifestation. It was part of a clue to hand the corrupt a review.

I had to cancel the method right through, trapping he who knew and he who had a clue. I was on the edge trapped in the middle of a test. It had me face a trace, create a piece so when I reach my limit, I could embrace another case to that method; that had me force my way in.

Breaking the cycle from within had me facing another

internal win. I had to feed off the trend that had me return and break the system with rhythm again. I was up to no good trapping those who rely on me to get by. It had me cave in on the concept and create a war in the corrupts peace.

Purely to get back on track and feed off the tremor that handed me a dilemma. I was handed a review. A challenge to skip that too, where I was given a presentation that took me in. Fed off me all while I was handed another review. A given a reason to escape and skip that too.

I was given a challenge that took me in. It gave me a second chance to repeat a new improved outlook. For I was on the move, on a journey that had me replace; following up on another case. Giving me the indication I was forcing my soul through. Interrogated by the corrupt final feud.

I had to feed off the energy that fed off me whole. It gave me a second chance to repeat hit back with a rebound. I had to fight an ending that trending then start again. But this time around the corrupt hit a dead end. They lose their light and their fight, handing me the reckoning.

They were on the move repeating just to cancel out another meeting. They created a war in my peace assuming that will break me. In fact; I needed a break it handed me the energy to be able to state a new fact create peace force my way in and present me with a new win.

Confirming the obvious, and that was I was hit with a trace stepped into a middle of a trend in the end. It broke the silence and I started again. Giving the corrupt a chance to pretend repeat rebel and create a challenge that will hand them hell. It gave me a chance to start a new alliance.

I had to free myself from a curse I can reverse. A past challenge that will serve me well and face me at the end of that spell. Where the corrupts method will give me the power to return, sit back, and devour. Handing me the entertainment that I needed to break the silence and succeed.

I came first, brock the cycle fed off the trial and hit back with a trace. I was served well at the end of that trend it forced me to return for a final vendetta. A trial an error and a faith less evolved but evolved it took me in and fed off me from within. A conclusion that was part of an evolution.

It was a key to break the silence and feed off the trend; it forced me pretend. For the corrupt had to redo and follow up on a review. Just to catch a glimpse of a future event. that took me in and fed off the trace that served me well from within. It was part of a release that had me feed off the beast.

It forced me to find peace after the fact. It had me face a trace, track down a case, break the cycle, and create a deception to that redemption. I had to follow up on a review feed off the concept and start new. Face a trace follow up on a fewest then when the time come; create a better outcome.

For that faith that had me foreclose another trace. Had given me a presentation that served me well at the end of that destination. For he who knew created the clue, it had me on the edge facing one more fear. Keeping up with the program gave me the trend to rebuild and start again.

It forced me to repeat and rebel against those who take me for granted. It had me follow up on a theme, handing me a vendetta in-between. It made me see the corrupt over-steep into the deep. It had me keeping up with the program. As I continue to redeem and create a brand-new theme.

It had me release that demon that forced me off the edge. A reminder I hit a final faith a trace that had me repeat another case. It caused an effect and forced me to return and resurrect. Presenting me with a trend that served me well and created a challenge that put me through hell.

I was taken to an infinite fidelity, just to catch up and face the corrupt. It an entrance that served me well. It handed me a spell caused an effect and faced me with a challenge that had me turned. It had me face a trace at the end of the race. Causing an effect, breaking a trend in the end.

I was served a strong wind and it broke my wing; at the nick of time. Then when the time come, I had to heal from that skill and reveal a trail an error and final dilemma. All while I overcome another outcome. I was taught a lesson, left to embrace that trace; then follow up on a brand-new vision.

It was part of a trace, that had me replace another case. I was given the freedom to replace the old start new and feed off the corrupt so I can get through. It was part of a past testimonial, a presentation to that manifestation that took me further than I thought.

Straight in to a journey that forced me to hit back with scrutiny. A trace, to feed off the trend, had me face another case; giving the corrupt a dead end at the end of that trend. I was to get in cancel the corrupts method leaving them hanging in there wasting every trap they left behind.

In the end I did not enter that ground up; I fell in contemplation and the lie gave me a chance to survive another dive. I had to make sure when I return and break the cycle the journey that caused the effects handed me a key to cave in on the concept and repeat after me.

It was of a presentation, that took me in and followed up on another win. I had to face the corrupts method so I can win and feed off the trace that handed me the treasure from within. I had to get in face another trace handing them a failure to project it with a final allegation to that manifestation.

I was forced to repeat and follow up on another trend. It gave me the entrance. It had me peak just before the corrupt could return for an encore. I had to break the trace follow up on another case. Heave at the concept trying my luck forcing whom ever to repeat a denial to that trial.

It handed me the evaluation, to give the corrupt a chance to confess; to that damnation. For they were returning for a curse they cannot rehearse it gave me a challenge that served me well at the end of that spell face me when the corrupt took me in and fed off me from within.

It was part of a terrible attack, where there fear of my presence took over and I felt the corrupt method crack undo and crumble to dust no more power to hit me and run. I had to face another unfaithful outcome. Where I could taste a sense of victory, at the end of that trend.

It served me well trying to cancel out a forthcoming spell. For they were wrong all along and because they made a huge mistake attacking me; It handed me a chance to get back on track and feed off the impact. It was giving the corrupt a chance to remove that groove at the end of that trend.

Feed off the energy that hit me at the end of that trend. I was faced me with a dead-end. Just to give the corrupt a chance to replace another case. A presentation that had me reaping a reward and following on a sacrament that had me on the raiding the heads of those who used me to get ahead.

I was to feed off the energy that had me replace the old and start new. All while I create a turn of events to feed off the corrupts method so I can claim my truth. I had to vent at the end of that trend. Keep up with the program, challenge he who knew and create an anomaly; so, I can get through.

I went straight into a trial an error and a final vendetta. It gave me a chance to return and follow up on another turn. It saw me an easy target faced me with a trace, followed me until the end of the race. It had me cover up on a trend that served me well in the end.

I was taught a lesson left to repeat then follow up on a reason; just to press delete. It trapped me just before I was hit with an encore. It had me on the go forced to repeat while I follow up on another trend it gave me a second chance to return and hit back in advance.

CHAPTER 6

◆ ◆ ◆

MY LEGENDARY STATUS REMAINED THE SAME

A stagnant affair that forced me to repair a trace; at face value. It had me facing my fear and follow up on a trace that had me on the edge of reason facing another treason. I was ready to repeat replace and face another way in; just to cancel out that freedom that served me a reason to win.

I was taken for a ride sped pass those who knew. Took a challenge that served me well right through. Taught a lesson ready to repeat and then when the time come press delete. I was to test that trace feed of the case takes a moment and replace. Give in to the corrupts method, then face the facts.

I was hitting a method that brought me forward, it faced me with a first and last competitive curse. So, when I reached my pinnacle, I can reverse the curse, take off, take a moment to break the silence, and present the corrupt with a cause and effect; breaking the system so I can resurrect.

It was to wrong a right, face another case; feed off the trace. A given power to redo and devour. I was to enter the corrupts realm face another fear get back on track and break the silence; so, I can resurrect. For each trace had me face another case; each force had me hit with remorse.

I was forced to hit back with remorse; it gave me a chance to repeat the same cause. I had to replace the old feed off the case, all while I give in and face another trim. I was trapped in the end, trying my luck to pretend. That is when I knew the corrupt had me face a waste.

I was tracking down those who tangle up and left a knot behind. It had me in knots forced to hit back with a lead to a place that had no ending insight it kept me dreaming living in drama facing another warning. Forced me into a yearning heaving. I was trapped; trying to get back on track.

I had to trace the case, hit back with a trend in the end. All while I get back on track and represent myself. For that one thing that had me face another win, was that trend that took me in. I was fed off me from within; it took me on a pathway that led me to win.

I entered without knowledge, a quick preview of what was to come next. It was the corrupts way of creating another contest. I was given a trace to lead me towards a trend. I had to replace a challenge that had me return for a fight. Lead me towards a journey that will serve me right.

I witnessed a lie just to give the corrupt another chance to get by. For the presentation was bland and I had no chance in hell of achieving another spell. I was given a free ride; on the condition I do not survive. Who put me in the position psyched me up for another competition.

I was handed a key that took me on journey that had a huge impact on me. That is when I knew I was silently on the mark, handing me a production of lost souls trying to evolve. I was getting back on track and presenting corrupt with a curse I can reverse.

That is when I knew the time had come; I had to overcome a failed attempt. It forced me to hit back with remorse following up on another cause an effect. I had no freedom nor foundation to reap a reward, for the journey was stagnant. It caused an effect and trapped me at the end of that threat.

It forced me to review, catch up, and finalise a damn trip down memory lane at a time. I had to face a trace; cause an effect and praise the corrupt just so I can resurrect. Meanwhile freeze the corrupts method follow up on a clue; face another fear so I can get through.

I was in the middle of a riddle, testing the patience of the corrupts second trail. It left me to repeat and follow up on a trend. The one thing that left me stagnant to my development in the end. For the time had come and I had to face another outcome. All while I give in and follow up on a break.

It had me on the edge violently supporting those who pledge. It gave me a second trial where the corrupt had me facing another debt at the end of that threat. It was part of a final review and a vague threat that had me win another dead end. It served me well and forced me to repeat.

For what I thought was part of the last resort. Gave me a second chance to hit back in advance. I was on the edge of facing a pledge, it gave me a prize-winning enterprise. I had to give in and feed off the concept from within. It forced me to repeat rebel while I face a trace at the end of the race.

I had to give in and face another trace presenting the corrupt a chance to hit back in advance I hit a journey and every time I was handed a review, a trace that became a faith less likely to undo broke the silence and forced me on the rise handing the corrupt another damn trace at the end of the race.

A premonition handed me a competition where I was given a chance to hit back with an invasion. I had to speak my mind and face another proposition to that proposition. For the imagination took over and I was fighting off another trace to that case it had me hit a trend at the end of that bend.

I was forced me to repeat follow up on another trace. It gave me a reason to rebel against the corrupt for no reason. All while the corrupt were trying to cover up another error. Where the journey had me face another tremor. Where this time around I am hitting back with a vendetta.

A concept that had me facing an invasion to that reservation. I had to step into a direction where I get in and resurrect at every manifestation. For all I knew I had no faith in the end of the race. I had to replace the old start fresh and repeat a challenge just to manifest another trace to that case.

I had an image that gave me a trend it handed me a poison to hit the corrupt with a passion. It was part of a trend that faced me in the end. If it was left to the imagination what would my life be like; if it all turned against me and I had no freedom or foundation to break that manifestation.

Releasing that demon that forced me to hit back with a fight took me on a journey that had me on the edge repeating a new improved meeting. It held me back and got me back on track. I fell into a trace that served me well at the end of the race. For I had to return to reclaim a debt.

It had me forced to replace the old and start new and face a fact. For what I had to do to get back on track had me feed off that review it handed me a second trial. It was a challenge to get me through and feed off the concept so I can get in run another inning. Then follow up on a brand-new theme.

For that trap had me overlap another way out. It forced me to repeat and face another doubt. I was warned I was about to hit a free ride. It gave me a second chance to hand the corrupt doubt. It took me on a journey that forced me to repeat. Then when I least expect it, return and press delete.

Giving the corrupt a chance to release and have me face another beast. It handed me redemption from that skill that forced me fully put me through hell. For the theme to that scheme had me relay messages in-between. It forced me to repeat and face another challenge at the end of that treat.

I had to rely on the corrupt to get by, it had me take the initiative face another redemption. Meanwhile cancel out that failed allegation presenting the corrupt with a method that had me reach my peak and follow up on another faith. One that had me reach my peak and break the silence.

Handing me the resolution to overcome another competition. It pushed me in the corner faced with a failed entrance. It had me haunted by the past, living in the present about to burst a bubble all so I never reach my pinnacle. I reached a point where every trace gave me trend in return.

It was part of a brand-new phase. I had to release a fierce challenge, that had me ace that case. Overcome a nasty outcome reach the end of my tither breaking the silence and facing another fear. Forced to repeat face another trace help me hit the corrupt with remorse.

I had to face what I assumed will follow me at the end of the race. Handing me the outcome I need to undo another review. I had belted the corrupt in the end of that route so when I reached my pinnacle, I can hand them fear. Forcing me to release that demon that caused me doubt.

It faced me with a faith less, likely to erase. It forced me to hit back and cause an effect. It had me follow up on a truth, so when I reach that point of no return, the challenge would be my first and last time to overcome that crime. It hit me when I went through it all it took me under that wing.

I lit up, fire took my shadow and saw me face another force; from the corrupt. One faith taken, one spirit forsaken one loaded gun and the world be taken. It had me softly, spoken reaching my pinnacle at every disposal. Where I was warned of what was to come from that outcome.

I went through the light and lit fire, burnt the corrupts kindle down. It lit a spark, broke the cover up. It had them facing a trace to that trend, led them to a dead end. It had me break the cycle in the end. For that trend was part of a given it had me power up and try my luck.

As I face the corrupt and hand them bad luck. I had to pretend then; I hit a dead end. Just to kick the corrupt off the raider so I can start again. Where every follow up gave me the last chance, to hit the corrupt with a final trance. A praise that had me face a trace; causing an effect.

It presented me with a curse that had me come first. It had me rehearse that feast that took over the beast. Handing me a farfetched after effect. For that dream that I was handed freely drama swerved through, ended in a nightmare. I could not see the light because I hit a faith less likely for me to fight.

I had to release that beast, handing the corrupt that final piece. For that next trace, handed me the closure to bring forth the beast. It forced me to replace and give the corrupt an everlasting praise before handing them poison. A new proposition caused an effect handing me a brand-new nest egg.

The next follow up had me facing another cover up. I was ready and willing to play the game. Little did I know I was facing the same fate. This time around I had no freedom to fight back. What I had become part of a trace that had me follow up on another trend in the end.

For the corrupt caused an effect; left me peruse and bemused. Ready to trap those who were forced to release that beast. It had me face another trace at the end of the race. I had refused to bath in a defiant full of shame. That had the corrupt return to hit back with another game.

Repeating a trace that served me well, then had me facing a fear now. Warning me that the scheme was part of a failed theme that; belted me in-between. It had me facing another theme forced to hit back with remorse. I was given a challenge, that had me return; with a faith less likely to eradicate.

I was forced to repeat, so the corrupts method can rely on me. Then feed off the concept one day at a time. Where this time around I get to free myself from another trace. Breaking the corrupts cycle so I can displace that trend that had me face another dead end.

I had to come through, overcome another review. I knew the trace was part of a case, that served me well at the end of the race. Where the road I was on took me in; forced me to overcome another win. I thought it would have faced me with a trace that caused an effect and left me intrigued

It had me recover like no other. It had me raise above and beyond. Where I was out of control trying my hardest to return and harvest. I was used abused, left to condition the mission adding to that proposition. While the rest followed by example, decided to hit me and run with a sample.

A simplicity to that complexity in the long haul; had come and gone. I had to run a musical in my head just to get ahead. Then when the time come overcome an outcome. A final review to help me get in settle the score and feed off the encore. It had me facing a trace, that forced me to repeat.

It had rebel against a warm scheme that created a theme in-between. It had me face another trace return for a thought to recover from that tremor. It had me work in solitude, against those who served me well. It presented me with a brand-new spell, face a trace; a third and final case.

Ready and willing to break that trend. It hit me God willing in the end. It had me first, foremost tie the knot get back on track reach my peak. Regaining conscious awareness again. So, when I reached the second and final hit, it became part of a physical game; forced to repeat; and remain the same.

It had me facing another trace, causing an effect trap me all while I get back on track. I had to feed off the trial the error and the final vendetta. It had me forced to rehearse and follow through to the next curse. Just to catch a glimpse of what was to come first.

It had me causing an effect at the end of the race. I was ready to burn, just to catch a glimpse of what was to come first. All so I can return and resurrect from that theme that had me return and scheme in-between. It had me feed off the concept, that had me face another win.

I had to fall, then rise above it all, in one setting. giving me the proposition to return for a new improved competition. I needed to protect my soul from feeding of that trend that had me face a dead end in the end. For that vision handing the corrupt a failed admission.

All while I continue to rise above and beyond; feeding of the edge of reason each and every season. So, when I hit the end the presentation, I could undo that reservation; that forced me to hit back. All while I give in breaking that chain an event that forced me to hit a dead end and a threat in the end.

I was handed a challenge and a brand-new manifestation. It became my way of accepting a challenge that had me fail; all before I hit that holy grail. It was part of a presentation that brought me forward. An end of that manifestation, where I was given a reason; to hit back with treason.

I was forced to undo and allow a follow up on a review just to get through. Hitting another review an indication I hit a manifested energy that ended in envy. Where every trace had me erase, following up on another case. Ready and willing to hit back with a chilling event.

It had me advert to an informal reasoning. It was leading me towards a journey that made me rise above and beyond. Warning me the strength to cause an effect had me carry on to the next threat. A debt that lined me up for a free ride to the other side. handing me the energy to skip that finally.

I had to schedule that feast that had me face another trace. Give into that feast that had me replace another final release. I had to overcome what I thought was part of an entrance to a long-term event. It had me replace what I thought was the resort.

It gave me a trend, that forced that will to survive another skill. It served me well in the long run. I was given a chance to hit back in advance, face a fear, force my way in, and prepare myself for another entrance. A non-win entrance; where every case had a second trial.

Every thought was part of a reasoning; it became my way of survival. I was entertained by the obvious, just so I can get in and feed off the trauma and the trend from within. It had me face a trace that forced me to embrace that case. A case that will hand me deliverance.

I was to give in, facing an ending of a statement of affairs. It had me wait for that trial and error to end. It sorted me out, caused an effect, and handed the corrupt doubt. In the end I was given a warning facing another trace. Only to witness, one thing; it left me trapped from within

It was part of an unprecedented trace; denying me access. It was the last draw, before I hit an encore. It was part of a trace at the end of the race. Giving me the indication I hit a brand-new resurrection to that manifestation. I had to get back on track and face an impact to that trend.

For the corrupt hit a dead end at the end of that trend. I had taught the corrupt the same old pace, to that space. It had me follow up on a trend that broke the silence. It fed off the concept, handing me the internal force, that faced me with a cause and effect. A challenge that held me to contempt.

I was to erase what I thought was part of the last resort. It had me give in and present the corrupt with a failed win. I had to trace that face, it had me case so when I hit the end of the race, I caused an effect and took that trail as an error and faced another delay to that dilemma.

For that competition reached its peak and fell into a repetition. It gave me a chance to revive, and follow up on another dive. All while I took it all in, and faced another traumatic event; from within. Handing the corrupt a failed attempt, giving me a chance to return hitting back; with extra flavour.

CHAPTER 7

◆ ◆ ◆

THOSE WHO KNEW AND DECIDED TO CLOSE THE DEAL

I was put in a position, that led me to a proposition; it had me facing another deception. I had to face a trace, kick a fuss, and put the corrupt through hell so I can catch them in the act; report them. With a fact! This time, leave a mark that had me face another case; cancelling their method.

I was given the freedom to face another trace. Handing the corrupt a reason to return for one more chance to break the silence and face another trace in the end of that case. All so I can condition the mission and follow up on another competition. I was given a reason to rise above the heavens.

It had me face another case accomplish a trend in the end. Where I witness a dead end and create a trial an error and a final vendetta at the end of that tremor. Handing me the foundation to repeat another manifestation. It was part of the corrupts challenge that took me in; fed off me from within.

It was I trying my luck to return and belt the corrupt with bad luck. It had me face another trace condition the mission and feed off the competition. I was stalling long enough to create a war in the corrupts trough. All so I can find peace at the end of that test that had me release that beast.

It forced me to create a lead at the end of that trend. I was to break the silence and feed off the trace, that had me face another case. All while I replace a trace that had me hitting another inning, it handed me a break in between. It was forcing me to return and hunt he who hit me and ran.

A challenge that took me in faced me from within; I was denial so I can get in and follow up on an inning. Where I decided to hit back and face a contraption at the end of that test that had me face another trace. Forcing me to break the silence and feed off the good deed.

Then in the mist, hire another trace to that case. I was served well, presented me with a final a stir to that incur. All so I can cancel that lead that had me face another trend in the end. For he who tried to get in to belt me like no other. Will face a feast, that will leave him suffering in-between.

All so I can face, the facts, lead the corrupt to a dead end at the end of that trend. Then when the time come overcome what I thought was the end of that outcome. But there was a conspiracy, under supervision, waiting to return and belt me at every mission.

I returned ready to feed off their vision. It was handing them failure and fear, where I take control and leave them suffering. The early rise became part of a late entrance. Where in the end I was served a presentation that will hand me the reservation; to force the corrupt out of that destination.

It led them straight into a composition; where the end, there was no competition. I made it to the end of my mission. I created the piece forced my way through hit a dead end and created new road. For that tradition become a violation to that manifestation.

It was handing me the reward to belt the corrupt at every beck and call. For those who were to subside, face a trace and feed off the concept; following up on another review. Just so I can catch up and break the cycle at every arrival. For that nonsense became part of a trivial pursuit.

I had to catch a break, face another tremor to that delayed vendetta. A dilemma that had given me a final trend became a festive result to season that had me reaching my potential leading me towards a journey that had me face another wrong to that trail that error and final vendetta.

For the trace became part of a visible game, it had me

face another trial in the end of that trend. It led me to break cycle again. It became a free ride to the other side in the end I had my chance to advance and follow up on another key. It was handing the corrupt a dead end to that conspiracy.

For the curse had me return for a final rehearsal. It became a faith less likely to rejuvenate. I was tracing a curse that had me break the silence at the end of the race. I had to erase the energy that had me fast forward to the next final case. It had me forced to repeat and fail another meet.

An entrance to that deception, handed me redemption. I had to look above and beyond the trace. It handed me a second trial; a given response that praised me when I hit the end of that stint. It served me an entrance, well deserved and desirable. It handed me a faith that forced me to repeat.

For what it was worth I thought it was last resort. It had me trying to face a formidable race. I was faced with an incantation to that foundation, forcing me to retake a deploy; at the end of that presentation. For the energy that handed me a curse, brought me forward.

I was to face a challenge to waste the corrupts time. Hounding me at the end of that trace had forced me to repeat replace and follow up on a trend. I had me return for a dead end. For that case gave me a proportion to that warning; that forced me to hit back with yearning.

My loss of faith to humanity had done me a favour. It gave me a second chance to release that beast. I had to face another case while the rest return for another test. An incantation to repeat and return the Favor, had me facing another dilemma. I needed to follow up on an executive decision.

One that had me face a competition. A trace that gave me the power to belt the corrupt at every divine colony. Where my survival technique, had me face an obligation to that rebellion allegation. Giving me the impression those who knew were trying to conspire with those who had a clue.

Where they were losing a competition. I was heading towards a favourable revision. For that manifestation had me face a release from that allegation. I had to give in and follow up on a competition just to raise awareness. It broke the silence that served me well at the end of that spell.

It had me on the edge serving me a purpose at every destination. It had me feed off the admiration that handed me an elevation to that wall that collapsed. I had to follow up on a trial and error then follow through towards another vendetta. A mission that broke the corrupts silence.

I had to devour that energy that had me divide and conquer another release. Rely on the corrupt, to get back on track, erase the trace and feed off the concept so I can clear the debt get back on track and feed off the impact. All while I follow up on a tradition to that mission.

When the time come, I had to undo that overload

of unnecessary information. For what the corrupt had created in my peace, had me on the edge facing another pledge. I had to review and follow up on another clue. It handed me threshold, where I get in and regain conscious awareness again.

I had no time to undo what the corrupt did over time. So, I decided the next best thing was harm he who harmed me to get in. It gave me a second chance to face another trace. I was to get back on track and follow up on another trend. So, when I reached to the top; I could start again.

This time around, I was faced with a condition that had me follow up on another competition. I had to renown and project what I thought was part of a trace that had me follow up on another case. It had me face a fear, where I decided the journey was one sided.

I did not expect to be treated with so much disrespect. I felt the journey unfold the trace evolve the trend take over and I face another wrong move. It had feeding off the impact. that had me sense the reality. That was society did not favour me whatsoever.

Whatever I did to achieve a goal, there would be another victim stating a fact. It had me getting back on track, facing an internal investigation. A bad omen to that final feast that had me retaliate at the end of that piece. Just to reveal that the method had forced me to revive another dive.

It had me get back on track remaining silent at the end of that trend. For what it was worth the trace was nowhere near the trend it had me repeating and regaining what I thought was part of a treatment that had me returning for another yearning. A thought pattern that became silent.

A respite, despite the expectation to that manifestation was part of a vision. It had me face another tradition at the end of the mission. It handed me the reason to return for one more treason. I was on the other end repeating an old wound. It had me stand my ground creating a challenge.

It had me forced to repeat and press delete. Because I was on the other end repeating that trace that had me starting again. The tend to overpower and start again had me feed off the trace that caused an effect and presented with a trail an error and final vendetta.

I had to feel the impact feed off the trace cause an effect and face another trend at the end of that final. It had me trace another trend at the end of that threat. It was part of trial that had me start again. I had to get back on track, face another fact then hit the corrupt back with an impact.

So, when the time come recreate another outcome. For whatever come my way there was always a lie to cover up the truth. That is when I knew I hit an ending that was pending and a challenge that was never ending. It was part of a trace to save me at the end of that race.

It had me follow up on a key, that gave me a second chance to release that beast. It forced me to replace, a challenge that rewarded the corrupt for the wrong reasons. It handed them a second chance to get back on track and belt me in advance. Releasing that demon that served me a treat.

I was given a reason to hit back with treason. For that concept at the end of that tradition had come and gone. It mended my spirit, handing me repetition. It had come to my attention I was handed a silent treatment assuming that will harm me; In fact, that is what had calmed me.

Then when the time come, hit back with an outcome; serving the corrupt a silent trace. I had to repeat remain vigilant to that trend. So, when I reached my pinnacle, I could start again. Just to follow up on a rumour, that had me facing another trial and error.

Giving the corrupt a dead end at the end of that trend. It had me face another trace. It was forcing me to repeat replace and face a trend at the end of that final condition a mission that had me accomplish competition. For what I thought was part of call back handed me a recall.

A case that had me remain silent again. Waiting for the trend, to release that beast that had me face another trace. All while I get back on track and praise that sentimental attack. It caused an effect and handed me the trial an error and a final vendetta. For all I knew there was no presentation to grasp.

Just a manifestation to hand the corrupt an ending that was pending. I had no freedom nor foundation to finalise that resting place. If anything, I was reassured that returning for a yearning, will pause an effect. It will give me the power to resurrect handing the corrupt a death threat.

It was part of a pointless affair, that served me well. It faced me with a challenge, that gave me a result that handed me the truth. I was given the freedom to back down and force me in, facing another trial and error from within. I needed to get back on track and face another impact.

It was part of a given, where the corrupt hit a final delay. It had me face a trace, giving me the power to undo and devour. Where I hit a forthcoming spell, where the trace will partition the mission. I will hit the corrupt with a petition undoing that tradition failing their mission.

I was to let go, set sail, and no longer waste another trace. Give in, to those who doubt and try their luck by handing me a whole lot of drama. There method was unworthy, there was trouble in the mist and I was stuck trying to force my way in; belting that trend from within.

It had me face a dead end, a method, that had me on the edge. Finally, in breaking the silence from within. There was a trace, that had me face another trend. A second trial so I can belt the corrupt from within facing a dead end to that trend. It was handing me the atmosphere to pretend.

I needed to accomplish a goal, just to get in and face another trend. When I hit the end of that trivia that handed me an and error. The trace had me face a tremor, hitting back with a vendetta. It gave me a superficial outlook to life. My troubles vanished and faith, over took the truth.

In the end I fell for the lie I overrode another wide-open event. An endeavour handing the corrupt a vendetta. A trend that served me well in the end. Giving me the impression I fell for that deception. All so I never lose, and the troubles that had me face a trace creating bad news.

Because every journey had me silent, it gave me a trace that served me well. It presented me with a curse I can reverse. I was hitting a trace, that had me rising above and beyond. I was stepping into a trap that had me raise the bar, all so I can catch up and face another trend at the end.

I was loaded with information; it handed me the confirmation; that served me wonders. It had me wording it in a way it was written in the long run. I was trapped in the middle of a condition. It served me well and saved me, before I was hit with repetition. It was all done under the raider.

It had me waiting, with a point taken, about to catch the corrupt hitting me and running. I was facing a trial, a failed attempt on the corrupts final revival. It had me face a trace that had me repeat a curse. I was presented with a key at the end of that verse; troubling the corrupt so I can come first.

In the end it gave me a chance to hit back in advance. It will give me the power to undo and devour hounding every momentum that served me a trace that had me face another curse about to reverse. All while I divide and conquer an energy to pretend and a trace to overpower a case.

I had to overcome a trace at the end of the race. It gave me the power to undo and devour. Where I get in and heave at, he who had it in for me. Entering the unknown and facing another trend at the end of that final dead end had me on the edge trapped ready to pledge.

I was to overcome an outcome. It had me face a curse at the end of that verse. I was put in a position where every comparison to that corruption had me face a proposition. In the end I was forced to undo and create an overview. Where the trend served me a curse that had me rehearse.

I was on the edge, faced with a pledge. Left to overcome an outcome. Where in the end I was taught a lesson, heave at the corrupts final reception. Always stay alert, face that trace hit the corrupt with a final pace. It had me face the truth state a fact and create a curse to get back on track.

It had me state a fact, trace a trend finalise that burn that took me in and forced me to break the cycle and start again. In the end of that trial and error. It forced me to hit back with a trace, all so I can erase. Then when the time come head on, heave and create a challenge that had me succeed.

I was given a faith less likely to succeed; it forced me to erase, then when the time come fail the corrupt at the end of that trend. I had to claim a chain reaction to the game. There were a time and a place for every case. For I hit the end of that trend, a trial that forced me to portray a bad day.

I was taught a lesson and left to return without handing the corrupt a chance to belt me in advance. It was part of a dead end at the end of the trend. For the corrupt were handing me grief. It gave me a chance to give in and face a trace at the end of the race.

It gave me a chance to hit back in advance, forcing me to feed off a trace. I was served an alliance at the end of the race. Causing an effect and feeding off the tread was finalising the end. It was handing me a treatment that had me curse that verse. In the end that had me request a confession.

For the patience of those who contest. Warned me; I hit a dead end. That is when I knew, the walls that were about to collapse at the end. It had me facing the facts, where I needed to get back on track and pretend that the feast was parting ways.

Handing me the trace that had me face another trend at the end of that final. It caused an effect and handed me an evaluation to that manifestation. It forced me to replace a case that had me trace another mission to that vision. I had to encourage he who faced me, then hit them with an interim.

Just to get the reaction, I needed to face him, was an absolute ghastly effect. I had to repeat a challenge at the end of that race. I was forced to hit back at the beginning of that case. Then cause an action that will hand the corrupt an abreaction that had me stepping into the unknown.

Releasing that demon that faced me at the end of that trend. I was taken for a fool, pushed in the corner, led to believe the drama was my fault. All so the corrupt can evolve, face a trace at the end of the race. I was forced hit back with a tremor then when the time come follow up on a heap.

CHAPTER 8

♦ ♦ ♦

SHOCK THE SYSTEM SO I CAN SURVIVE ANOTHER MISSION

I was taken for a fool, left to repeat just to catch the corrupt in deceit. A trace to that case became versatile and I hit a method that was presented with a key. Handing the curse that I needed to return and reverse. It had me face a trend at the end of that trace; that served me well.

It caused an effect and created a trend, where I had to break the cycle and start again. Giving in was part of the win, fighting back had me facing a trace to get back on track and erase the case. I was trying my luck, where I could bribe the corrupt again.

I had no choice it was part of a key, just so I can get back on track and face another dead end. For the corrupt at the end of that presentation handing me a validation to that cause an effect. I had to catch up and feed off the facts trace that test and face another trace at the end of the race.

It served me well at the end of the race, preventing the corrupt from stating the facts. It had me face a dead end that took me in and replaced me at the end of that trend. For those who had me break the silence, released a feast. It forced me to face the facts; erase the case and get back on track.

It forced me to release, then in the end of that trend find peace; a follow up on another feast. For every pass took me in, heaving at me at every whim. I had to face a trace, cause an effect, and feed off the death threats. It had me form an alliance on my own, where I hit a free ride.

It created a challenge I could not divide, for every trace had me face a subdivision; to that mission. For the concept was changed and the trend was too hard to blend. The project, became part of an invasion that handed me a trace; it served me purpose at the end of the race.

All because every journey had sent me a rejection letter. In the end I went out ventured out on my own, where everything that had me face a trace stirred the pot and created a final feast at the end of the race. It had me finalise that step into a direction I could not convey.

Unless I had a free ride to override a trace; the end of the race will close early. It will hand the corrupt a handicap so they never trace nor even attempt to cover up another mistake. For that case nor even a came to my attention the trace was part of a redemption.

It had me follow up on a clue, just so I can cave in on the concept and screw he who knew and belt he who had a clue facing me with a trace that forced me to incur another stir. For every challenge stepped into a direction, that handed me a manifestation to that deception.

Every trace, handed me an anomaly. It made me see beyond unity and tranquillity. For whatever was meant to be; gave me a chance to return and hit back in advance. Handing me the opportunity to create a raw rude awakening. A journey to reclaim a division to a game, that made me step forward.

I felt the energy override that trace, it had me face another case. It gave me a rude awakening a follow up to the next key. A gamble that gave me the trend that served me well in the end. I had to override and subside to the next level and the case come to an end forced me to pretend.

It had me facing one more key just to follow up on a challenge that served me wrong. For I was handed a trace that served me well at the end of the race. Then when the time come, hit back with a challenge that will hand me a clue. Forcing the corrupt to face another review.

I was given a challenge that served me well. It forced me to review and follow up on a clue. Because I was to forgive, forget and catch up on the corrupts method. It had me face another trace; it had me trace a trend, that took over that service that had me repeat another trace in the end.

For that case forced me to repeat, replace, and follow up on a condition to meet the corrupt half way. Only to witness the trace was based on a condition that forced me to repeat another mission. I had to feed off the vision, and create a deception to that coercion.

It was part of my resurrection, that took me in and faced me from within. Just to catch up and follow through to next manifestation. For the outlook that took me in, fed off me from within. It had me face another trace. I was taken for a ride at face value. A break in-between the two worlds.

It served me well and brought me forward, where every trend had me break the silence in the end. It took me forward and had me face another trace. Where I took the journey and forced me to follow up on a trend that had me break the trace and the silence in the end.

It failed me, when I hit the energy that was provided to me. For I was given a chance to hit back in advance. It was my way of trying to get back on track and feed off the impact. It served me well at the end of that trace. It had me fast forward and replace that case that served me well.

For I was left to intrude in the vision of the corrupts

final opposition. I had to endeavour to replace another vendetta. before I am forced to pass a test. It gave me a second chance to hit back in advance and face what I thought was part of the last resort.

I was given a challenge that will serve the corrupt well, if I did not follow up on another route. I would be stuck in a rut, chasing the wrong feeding off the weak, so I can remain strong. It will hand me an invasion to sweeten the deal and create an entrance that will face me right through.

The case closed early, and forced me to rise, I was handed a vision to claim another competition. I had a choice; I had to repeat overcome the loss and release that beast. Just to teach the corrupt a valuable lesson. Not return the favour but them their place most defiantly.

Never will they speak in tongue, nor ill hearted of me again. Because my tongue will warn them and the hand that they dealt with will hand them a guilt trip that will turn their world into a fire. Enter from the soul where they will never see their spirit rise above that hole.

For that generation gap, had come and had gone, just as quick. It had me face another challenge that took me in and forced me to hit back with a final win. It was part of a challenge that fed off the trend that gave me a trap that forced me to repeat and replace another dead end.

For the light took me in and faced me from within. It had me face another treasure to that measure. It caused an effect and faced me at the end of that debt. It led me to ease the pain, serve the corrupt a challenge at the end of that domain. It created a journal of upcoming events.

It had me cave in on the concept and try my luck, all while I continue to break the cycle and feed off the corrupt. I had a trace method that taught me how, just to give the corrupt a chance to fight back in advance. A forthcoming spell that gave me a trial an error and a forthcoming tremor.

I had to live and let live, start fresh and break the energy that left me to repeat a trial to that mile. It had me face a warning that had me hit with a yearning, it brought me forward and trapped me with a curse that faced me at the end of that verse. Warning me I had no chance in trace to that case.

It had me creating a new journey in advance, where I was given a reason to break the silence. It had me face another treason. It had me return for one reason and that was to hit back with a fusion to that mission that gave me a brand-new spanking vision.

I had to face a verse to that curse, repeating what I thought was the last restoration to that manifestation. In the end of that trend that forced me to repeat and rebel against those who put me through hell. For what I thought I was given the energy to hit back with the last resort.

It had me face a fear, to that journey, that had me repeat and rebel against those who saw me easy. They made me out to be an easy Target. Warning me to play there way because I was their victim all the way. It had me face another trace step into the unknown just to give in and feed off the inning.

I had to follow up on a tremor and then the drama that followed from within. It had me step into a final feast, that gave me the power to find peace. It had me gamble one dream after the next, in the end I gave in and prayed to God from within that every trace that followed will end.

Forcing me to embrace a trace a loss of every trough. A triumph that took me in at every trial error and every final vendetta. For the trend had me face a dead end. For those who knew, wanted to enter my realm face me then attempt to enforce a cause of action to that abreaction.

Those who assumed the trace was part of an entrance, took me in. For that method had me entitled to an expense that warned me I was nowhere near I was meant to be. For that final vendetta, handed me an ending that was pending and a trial that was never going to come to fruition.

I kept losing a battle but winning the war. That is when I knew, I hit a long-term effect of a trail an error and a final delay to that vendetta. It was part of an error an event an everlasting vendetta. For what I assumed had me hit an expense took me in and fed off me from within.

For they could not refine, or even return for one more trace. I had to bend over backwards just replace that case. I had to serve those who did not deserve my presence. For that case that had me embark in a brand adventure. For I was led on led to believe where faith took over.

It faced me with a lineup of threats at the end of those debts. It gave me the impression the loyalty to that manifestation, was based on a case; it had me break the silence. For the system and the trace that handed me a brand-new vision was replaced; I on a merry-go-round of spontaneity.

Where every trace, had me replace that trend; that had me start fresh again. For I was given a reason to hit back with treason a faith that taught me a lesson at every trace. It had given me a reason to report those who enter and try to feed off the date that caused the wrong effects.

It created an entrance that served me well, it poisoned the corrupts spirit and put me through hell. A method that took me in had me face a reason to hit back with treason. I had to find the energy to define that crime that had me follow-up on a trace; that had me face another case.

I had to revive, follow up on a trace, it had me dive into a challenge; it caved in on the concept. Then when the time come unwrap another outcome and trap those who violate at the end of that trend; it had me start again. I was given a reason to hit back, and follow up on a new development.

A position that had me hitting back with repetition. Caused an effect and handed me an evaluation to the next final reservation. I was taken back, forced to hit back all so I can claim another division to the game. Where I was about to gamble a trace that had me erase another key.

It had me facing a warning, that led me towards a journey. It had me face another trace and finalise the energy that had me compete compel and face another forthcoming spell. I had to separate the two, so I can skip that too, then when I least expect it challenge, he who knew.

It had me creating a trend, that will help me foretake another trace; in the end of the race. Where the only thing that come my way. Will be a new door opening, along the way. It had me on the verge of presenting the corrupt with a pledge. It had me on the edge stirring the pot again.

It had me breaking the silence and forcing my way in. It brought me back to reality; a civilised society non-existence. I had been forced to strengthen that presentation. Pretending that the challenge with a never-ending battle. For the clue was part of the revue it handed me an ending that was pending.

For all I knew nothing was given nothing was taken and every journey was forsaken. I was involved in a trace that had me break the silence at the end of the race. It had me face another internal investigation. I was taken for a full left to trace that trend that handed me an evaluation.

I had to regain conscious awareness; forced to review

and finalise that clue. It had me face another trend at the end of that final bend. I was on a path that broke that wrath, where I had to follow up on a key that served me well at the end of that forthcoming spell. Forced to hit back with remorse.

It had me rebel against those who knew. It gave me a second chance to hit those in advance. For those whom were troubled were to be replaced. Because the corrupt saw me as an easy target wanted me to face another trend at the end of that cycle. that forced me to pretend in the end.

For he who had a clue had me prepare for another review. It had me fall onto a journey that had me relive another lie just to get by So, when I reached my pinnacle, I had to raise the buck rise above that bad omen. Then follow up on another trough. I had to repeat rebel and face another channel.

I had to attend a bribe, that did not make sense in the end. For the corrupt were handing me a fine, a trace that will give me the trend; that will serve me well in the end. For I was given a true reality to that spontaneity forced to hit back with a trace that had me get back on track.

For I was given a true reality to unprecedented event. It brought me forward and faced me with a debt. For I was given a truth that gave me the opportunity to release the beast. It had me face another tremor, just before the corrupt returned for another vendetta.

It was part of a second chance, to release that beast and

face another feast. I had to catch up on what I call a recall. While I get back on track, trapping those who invade in my privacy. Assuming their method will bring forth peace. In fact, all it did was return repeat and hand me a key.

I was left to restore, undo the trend once more, with a conscious awareness. A trade that will help the corrupt succeed and hand me the faith that will lead me to a destination that will hand me a resurrection. I had to follow up on a clue, because the corrupt attempted to mind read me.

It had me on the edge, reaping a reward and stating a new fact. All so I can return and repeat a new lead. It had me face a trace, step into an unprecedented event. It took me in, where I was taken by surprise from within. I was harmed from one end and to the next faced with a dead-end.

I was taken for a ride, to replace the old with the new. An energy that served me right; right through. I was handed a key, branded with an intention that took me in. It faced me with an evaluation that trapped me from within. It had me facing a force to be reckoned with and a chance to win.

A trend to descend had come it led me to the end. A presentation to accompany me to the next destination. I was on the mark, trapped in the middle of a deception that handed me redemption. I was given a reason to hit back with treason. Meanwhile trap the corrupt with a competition.

I was torn in more than one direction; it handed me the presentation. I was held up and handed an evaluation. A beginning of an expense that had me rise above and beyond; it had me returning for a favour so I can remain strong. I was heading for a fall waiting to regain a conscious awareness.

All so I can start again, it was part of a given. A chance to release that beast, I was faced with another trace at the end of the race. It was handing me the truce, that gave me the power to reduce. I was left to embrace another travesty to that theme that gave me power in-between.

I was trapped in-between, left to embrace another trend in the end. Reaping a reward and starting again. All so I can give in and repeat another win from within. For he who tried to repeat took me in and fed off me from within. Trying there hardest to harvest, all while the rest were stirring the pot.

I was at the end of my tither regaining conscious awareness again. It had me creating a feast that had me return and replace another beast. For that curse had me reverse handing me the evaluation to help me come first. I was led on, given a promotion to remain strong.

It had me face a fear, grasp for air, create a test and repeat; whatever come my way. Just so I can remain vigilant and stable from that fable. I was returning for one more yearning. An energy to release that beast. It had me face another trace forcing me to return and catch a wave.

I was to trade in for an expense; just to win that inning.

I was led on creating a chance to hit back in advance. I was to hit a dead end, a threat so I can I rise again. He whom had seen me as an easy target had me refined. A follow up on a trace, an end to that race; preparing me for one more case.

CHAPTER 9

◆ ◆ ◆

WHEN THE TREND HITS A DEAD END & THE CORRUPT FACE A FAILED LEGISLATION.

Where do I begin? How do I get in? When do I make it happen? The trace had me face another trend in the end. I was landed a role, heaved and fell into trace that served me well. It gave me a free ride, to the other side. I was given a presentation to rise above the occasion.

Handing the corrupt damnation to that manifestation was part of a reflection to that divination. It was part of a deviation that handed me an evaluation. It had me face another informal investigation. It led me towards

THE TEMPLE OF ZEAL

a journey that had me state a fact, handing me a challenge to get back on track.

It gave me a chance to divide and conquer, for a new theme became part of a scheme. It had me face another trace release a beast, then when the time come fast forward to next entertainment. I had to follow up on a theme break the silence in between.

It had me enforce a new cause of action, delaying every trace that took me in and faced with a vendetta that served me well from within. I was left to embark in brand new task then when the time come overcome another outcome. It faced me with a trend that had me forced to pretend.

It took me in and broke the silence from within. I was led on, led to erase and follow up on a journey that had me facing another trend, at the end of that final dead-end. I had to focus on a tremor that served me well at the end of that terrible attack a trace that took me in and faced me from within.

I was led on, left to strut on my own, and remain strong. That intimidation to that evaluation forced me to revive and follow up on another dive. I was taken in, left to repeat and follow up on an entrance to a manifestation that had me relive another method to that curse about to reverse.

I had to reconsider the facts, catch up, and face another trace. I was handed an inner response to that trace that had me face another failed attempt at the end of that debt. I had to follow up on a review give in and feed off the trace that caused an effect and forced to erase that case.

I had to feed off the energy that had me face another threat. It had me state a fact get back on track and present the corrupt with a trace that served me well at the end of race. Because I was given time to heal, they put me on the road to recovery. Facing me at the end of that trinity.

I had to face another tremor to that vendetta. It took me on a journey that warned me. I was no longer forced to hit back with remorse, nor given a reason to face a vision. For that component that saw me as a victim, assumed hitting me and running will hand them the forthcoming.

I was taken for a fool, stalling long enough to reward he who was yearning for my company. For I was given a reason to hit back with a brand-new development. An opportunity to release that beast that had me awarding those who follow up and hit me with a round up.

For that redemption that handed me an evaluation served me well. It had me face another upcoming spell. I had to revise and claim another truce to that game. It was part of a trace that had me face that reserve. Meanwhile it caused an effect and brought solitude to my resurrection.

I was headed for a fall, left to repeat and remain silent. All so I never fail another trace to that case. It brought me forward and took me in it dedicated my validation that served me well from within. I was cursed with a verse that denied me access. It took me in and fed off me from within.

I was presented with a key that left me to ordain to another game. I had to embrace another case. So, when I reach the end of that trend, I will be given a reason to embrace another trace. A case to cause an effect and break the silence so I can resurrect and have me follow up on another debt.

I was given a reason to hit back with a trace; it had me facing a component. I had to remain silent embrace a case feed off the energy that had me force to hit back with remorse. On the event I give in and break the silence from within. I was on the edge, repeating an event that led me astray.

It gave me a trace that forced to embrace a case. Then when the time come overcome another outcome. I had to face a trace give in and follow up on another win. All while I trace that trend and trick the corrupt in the end. It was part of a challenge that served me well.

It gave me the opportunity to repeat rebel and push the corrupt in the corner. All while I give in catch that praise that handed me a dead end at the end of that trend. I was to face another dead end. I had to rebel and find my way out of that hell. It gave me a chance to hit back in advance.

Reassuring me that cause of action, was based on a final abreaction. That internal investigation, handed me an entitlement; a need to hit back with scrutiny. A case, in the end, where the trace will become part of an evolution. It handed me a review giving me the power to skip that too.

It became a faith less likely to erase and a challenge that gave me a forceful event. It led me to a destination that hit me when I hit the end of that trial. An investigation that pushed through feeding off the trace that served me well it forced me to repeat rebel and face another spell.

In the end of that trend, it caused an effect, and embraced that chase. It took me in and fed off the energy that had me face another lead to that method that had me succeed. I had to follow up on a debt. Where in the end of that recording it forced me to repeat, deny access and press delete.

For I was dismissed and led on. Just to convey another bad day. I had to follow up and delegate a momentum, at the end of that manifestation. It had me face another resurrection to that next feast. A damnation to the next foundation. Where the end of that trend handed me a dead-end.

I hit the end of the race handing me the opportunity to hit back with a valid response. The one thing that will hound me to hit the corrupt facing another force. Feeding off the trace that had me face another trend in the end of that upcoming event.

I had to claim a condition get back on track and feed off the competition. It handed me a validation to next final manifestation; it took me in and fed off me from within. I had to frame those who took me in and failed me periodically. I had to claim a game create a piece and face another feast.

I forced my way in, took a wrong turn then decided the journey from within will hand me a definition that will break the silence and heave from a trace from within. I will face an evaluation that will have me face another trace. For I was given a position to claim the trend at every position.

I was left to release, cave in on the concept and press delete. I had to delay and follow up on a game, that had me face another trace. I Burnt the script and warned of what was to come from that outcome. It had me facing another condition feeding off the proposition.

That journey that ended in tragedy, gave me a chance to get back on track. I had to follow up on a test then try my Luck, while I step into a journey and feed of the trough. It handed me a yearning then process towards a conquest. That energy that created the piece; it had me focused on the old.

For the new had me overcome an outcome. The old had me face a trace and the foundation to start fresh, took me on a journey that led me on. It gave me the impression that every trace was imperishable. It handed me a challenge that served me well at every case.

It was giving me the impression, the only trap that left, had me open to discussion. It was the one thing that had me raid the heads of those who hit me and ran from within. I was faced with a condition that served me well at every deception. It caused an effect trapped those who resurrect.

It was part of a mission that handed me a conclusion. It forced me to hit back with a resolution. Giving me the impression, I hit the end of that damnation. A presentation that served me well and handed me incursion to that trace. It pushed me through; holding on to one more clue.

It had me face another dead end; overcome a trace to that trend. It hit me cause and effect catching up and accusing those who hit me and ran. It forced me to face another break to that trade at the end of the case. It was handing me the entertainment I need to resurrect.

I was served well presented with a forthcoming spell. It had me survive a dive. In case I was not able to see beyond what I thought; it was a task to hand me the last resort. In the end I had no chance in hell of repeating, I was spoilt with choice. I had to many in the meeting trying to cover up a feast.

A new spell had caused an effect it had me reopen a case. It had me force to open an old case and bring it all out in the open. Then close that trace that had me face a disgrace. It was part of a staged play; dramatizing every step of the way. It handed me redemption, that had me face a fact.

A cave to that stave, it had come to be, it led me on and faced me in the long run. It had me face another final degree. I weas on the edge, trapped in the middle of a pledge. I was on the move trapped in the middle of a dead in on the concept and erase the case that had me evolve.

I was stepping into the young, the old and the pretty. It had me on track surviving, another warning. In case path ended in my favour. It was part of a journey that will bring me forth. A challenge that had me repeat and follow up on a trace to that case. I was repeating a given momentum.

For the opportunity to press delete, rose and I was on the other end. I had to face an edge preventing the corrupt from returning for a yearning. For I was given an opportunity to trace a trap fast forward to the next impact. I was heading towards a trend that handed me a challenge.

It had faced me with an ending that served me well. It was handing me accomplishment, to grab what I ever I could then run with it. I had to feed off that raw and replace it with an upcoming roar. I needed to skip hell, try my luck, feed off the corrupt. As I make the world at large listen; to who?

That Demon that forced me off the edge, or the Angel who lifted my spirit when I was pushed. I was hit me with a lie, all so I can pledge. I was given a chance to give the corrupt an opportunity to redeem themselves. What good would it have done, if I gave in and handed the corrupt a non-win.

I was to reserve a trace that took me in and faced me from within. I had to accomplish a serve, just to find peace from within. So, when the time come, I could return for another outcome; one that will work in my favour. I had forced the old the new and the energy to follow up on another review.

I was forced to break the silence, hit back with an alliance. I was given a challenge risen above and beyond, giving me the opportunity to embrace a trace. I was taken for a true rude awakening that had me curse that verse. I was hit back with an expense that took me in and fed off me from within.

I had to face another trace, a given reason to hit back with treason. I had to follow up on a key, then when the time come face another final degree. It had me face a demon that will help me retrieve and revive another dive. Torn at every direction, waiting for the corrupt to return for one more hit.

A retrace to the next final case; became final. Given a momentum to hit back with a delusion. A given impression I hit a deception. Just to trace that certainty at the served me well at the end of that trend. Where the race improved, with an embrace a curse that will help me come first.

I was given a method that served me well, it gave me a chance to delve into another trance. A thorough investigation had me face another interrogation. Seen as I was a victim of a no show, it became evident I was being used and abused; I was left to refuse to become a muse.

I refused to accept their bribe; where my key was stolen.

forced to survive in drainage; drowning in sorrow. It handed me feeding off the clue return for one more review. Just to give in breaking the silence from within. I was to lose my light, then a fight; so, the corrupt can return for one more bite.

Just to give the corrupt a chance that took me in and face me from within. It had me face a trace give into to that case. I was taught that lesson left to entertain my soul; with the impression I was on the road to making it happen. I was torn in more than one direction waiting to return for a deception.

I had to take that trend and fed off the drama in the end. I had to harm and follow up on a review. It took me in and faced me from within, lending me the harm that served me resurrection to that deception. I was taught a lesson it had me face another trace to that case.

It had me trace, that case that caused an effect. It broke the silence, at the end of that deception. Leading me towards the wrong direction. It had me reaching a popularity contest. It was part of a trace, that brought the corrupt down. Straight into a final feast, that took me past the old.

It created the new, I was led to face a trace. It gave me the door to a new flaw, an honour that will hand me a clue one more. It had me creating a challenge that will help me get through. It caused an effect trapped me in the middle of that defect. So, when I reach my peak, I could undo it all.

I was to replace it with a clue, trap he who knew,

then the time come catch a break. I had to feed of the outcome. A trend that had me fast-forward to the end and start again. I was given a reason to break the system feed off the treason that served me a reason just to follow up on a new treason.

The only thing that brought me joy, was the journey that become surreal. I was given a reason to establish another treason. It was part of a pathway to the unknown. Where I did not have the right angle to return and scheme another theme. Because I hit the extremity in-between.

Outstretched, undone, and finalised by the outcome. I was watching the corrupts failure, and it was handing me joy. Every trace, took me in and faced me with a curse that will save me and free me from a trend that had me cause an effect; while I regain conscious awareness again.

It became part of my saviour and every time I was given a chance to set sail the only thing that faced me from within was the challenge that served me well. It helped me get in and win everything. for every trace had me lead the pact. It gave me the entrance to get back on track.

Leaving them trapped and nowhere to sail. Warning me the trace was better than the energy that took me through to the next review. It had given me the opportunity to remain vast to that spell; it had me casted for a role that was meant to be removed from society.

I was given a challenge that had me face another return. I had to scheme then follow up on another trace. It had me redeem that one thing that brought me forward. I was faced with a challenge that had me retreat return and feed off the choice that had me rejoice.

I was handed one more scheme, rising to that trace that forced me to undo and replace another kind heart to that trace that served me at the end of the race. It had me face another case, it gave me the royalty, needed to travel to the next. A final unravelled event; that revealed the truth.

I had to look forward, lead the pack, and repeat rebel and get back on track. It was the trace that served me well it gave me the foundation to push the corrupt through hell. That one that will bring peace had me look forward, towards a journey that was about to open the door to war.

I was on board, on the road to you know who, warning me the trace will hand me a case. It was forcing me to replace the old the new and the conspiracy that threw me off track and screwed me right through. It had me take a moment to replace them; with a curse I can reverse.

All I had to do was come first, retrieve the old, revive the new compete with he who knew. I had report those who had a clue handing me the power I need to get through. Where the troubles were handing me unity. It was part of a trace that served me well. It became a pointless affair.

It brought me to my knees, serving me praise to that trace; that caused an effect. I had to enter without notion I had to release that beast then upstage those who used me to get in and then have them surrender to those who knew forcing me to return for one more review.

CHAPTER 10

♦ ♦ ♦

A FAILED REDEMPTION A CLASSIFIED REJECTION

When the corrupt return for redemption, but I am classing it as a classified rejection. All while I get in and uplift that energy that had me face another resurrection from that deception. I was left to award those whom were harming me. Handing them resolution and harmony.

A task that was harming me, had my spirit rise above; charming me. Each occasion handed me a task served me a true sense of relief. I had to feed off the concept, that had me restore what I thought was part of an everlasting piece. I was to release; facing a keynote, a test that will break the silence.

I was given a key, a follow up on a written report. Taken for granted, left to release. Taught a lesson for good and above all a willing to fight back and face a faith less likely to eradicate. In the end of the race the case will erase handing me the invasion that will serve me well presenting with a curse.

I was taught a lesson left to reproduce; I was taken on a journey that had me rely on the corrupt to get by. It had me release that beast. Left to hit back with a forsaken Identity. It took me on a pathway that had me refined. It trapped me in the middle of the divine.

I was taken for granted greeted with a gift hit with a disadvantage taken for a ride and left to reminisce a future condemnation that will leave me facing another trace to that case creating a piece, that will lead me to a destination that will harm the corrupt at every reservation.

It was part of a challenge that will help me refine another feast. I had to skip another trip down memory lane. A pathway of the divine forcing me to renew and face another game. It was handing me a clue so I can remain the same; hitting the corrupt at the end of the game.

I had to trace that case at the end of the race; causing an effect. It was breaking the silence so I can resurrect. For the intention was evil, I had to unveil another safety net to that scheme that had me break the silence in between, it had me chase and face another trace.

I was served well; it gave me a chance to get back on track. It was forcing the corrupt to hit back and face another trace at the end of the case. Handing me the incantation to hit back with an informal investigation. I had to follow up on a key and face another trace hitting back with unity.

The journey was case closed and I was led to believe that every dream created an anomaly. It led me on forced me to remain strong so when I hit the end of that trend. Each momentum will bring forth peace and the energy to release a burning desire to light a flame; causing an effect.

I had to face a challenge at the end of that threat. For those who encounter and feed off the entrance to that deception at the end of that redemption will hand me a final lease to life releasing that demon that had me fight back returning the favour to get me back on track.

I was led to believe that each method had me succeed. I was forced to replace the old at the end of the race. I had to invade validate and trace that case that had me repeat an interaction to that redemption. Face me at every violation. I had to follow up on a gift; that had me face a trace.

I had to follow up on a reward then when the time come hit back with a trace. A trap to restore my energy and get back on track and erase. Just to release that beast that handed me a redemption at the end of that destination. I was taught a lesson relcase where I took the initiative.

It held me up and harmed me at every final conviction.

It took me on a pathway where the motivation served me a sentence. It forced me to relive following up on a mission. I was thrown of the deep end. Held up, and forced to return feeding off what I thought was part of the last resort.

It held me up helped me find peace at the end of that trend that forced me to repeat. I had to Start fresh regain momentum from that redemption. I had to gain revolution to that manifestation that took me on a path based on rhythm an exhibition to that mission that served me a composition.

I was to elevate from trade, straight into a redemption relying on competition. I had to follow up on trick of the trade. It had me stalling long enough to repeat, remain silent and press delete. It handed me the motive that brought me forward an impression the invasion was part of the foundation.

It had me take the initiative face a revelation from that destination. It was hitting me every time I was given something to think about. I was taught a lesson trapped in middle of a conviction trying my luck to hit back with a curse I can reverse and a challenge to help me come through.

I was repeating another overview to that review. Creating a warning that served me well it forced me to revive and survive another spell. I had to face another trace and follow up on a verification to the next destination. It forced me to review and create an over view

I had to chase a case, forced to repeat and replace. When I hit the end of that trend, I could overcome, start again, feeding off the trace, that was part of a release. It hit me at the end of that trend that created a final dead end. A case that had me entertained by the notion.

Where every trend met me at face value. It created a divided attention to that redemption. I was handed an extension to that redemption that forced me to overcome a final test. A given chance to help me get back on track and create a challenge that had me face another feature to that case.

I was handed an entrance to an expense. It forced me to replace a case at the end of that trend, facing another release to that beast had me follow up on a journey, I could not review. I was taught a lesson in advance, just to retrain my moral once again.

I was taken for a fool, taught to review another clue. It had me on the edge returning for one more review. It had restored my truth and my energy that followed through. I was taken in and fed off whom ever just to follow up on a return. It took me in and fed off me from within.

It had me face a true reality. It gave me a sense of amity; forced me to find peace. Just so I can claim another division to the game. I had to redo and repeat a new feast. A case that served me well at the end of the race so I can release and find peace. A presentation that led the corrupt towards the vital.

A minor inclusion, to that delusion had me face

another entrapment to that entitlement. It was giving me the impression that I was being entertained by the interrogation that handed me refusal to that informal investigation. An interaction that served me a resurrection; from that deception.

It handed them a lesson that will starve them of resurrection. Assuming the worst was behind us, in fact I was entertaining them so I can release the beast and come first at every piece. A turn of events created a conspicuous amount of energy; just to feed off the synergy that had me reputed.

I was put in a position where the corrupt were invading my privacy. I had to return reclaim and follow up on another game. It gave me the energy I needed to repeat a past trace to a case that had me follow up on a review. I had to repeat fight back, press delete; only to witness I hit eyewitness.

I had to follow up on a clue repeat a review then when the time come return the favour threefold. For the outcome, had me state a fact. It had me face another case close the trend and break the cycle in the end. I had to cave in on the morose, so when I reach my pinnacle, I could impose.

I had to indulge, then give in to what I thought was part of the last resort. It had me release then find peace; all in one setting. Where I was given the impression, where the interaction was worse than the mission. I was left to hit back with a competition. Because the task became part of an invasion.

It was handing me the interpretation, that served me an expense. It had me return for another confirmation. It fed off me at every proposition, handing me the interval to that interaction. I was taught a lesson a given impression, trapping me at every pathway.

For the journey that served me well at the end of that mission; Became poison. I had to release that beast that forced me to find peace. Where my interpretation landed me a role that handed me an invasion to that composition. It forced me to repeat catch up and find a way to break the silence.

For that trace had me face another case, giving me the impression I hit a deception. It had me forced to open one door and shut another. A trend in the end of the race returning for one more case to erase. Warning me every thread of redemption, will hand me revision.

Giving me the impression I hit a final reservation to that paradox. I was taught a lesson left to release that beast forced to hit back, break the silence; to get back on track. My patience ran thin; it was part of a test where my freedom to resurrect was gifted from within.

So, when I reach my limit, I stay alert and follow up on another feast; to that beast. I hit back with an invasion to that manifestation. Warning me every trace and every challenge served me a condition that led me to a competition; that taught me a valuable lesson.

I had to release that beast face another feast catch up and finalise the corrupt. I had to see if the trace had given me the impression to fight back with recognition.

For my intuition took over, and the only way to get through was embrace another clue. For fighting back was not part of the review.

Intruding in the corrupts final repetition, handed me the vitality; a need to restore my energy. I had to feed off the trace that had met me informally alleged with another pledge. It gave me a warning that had me face another yearning. Reminding me I hit the end of that trend that had me start again.

I took it all in, fed of the trace that had me face a dead end in the of that trend. I had to follow up on a review catch a break and face another case. It was part of a condition that had me repeat another mission. I was on the run, consciously unaware waiting for the corrupt to return and roughen me up.

It had me on the run reminding me I was hit a long-term effect of traps. In the end of that trace, that served me well. I was given a challenge that handed me a review, it forced me to look back and break the silence so I can get through. It had me replace the old the new and the forthcoming clue.

Taught a lesson; a chance to power through. It forced me to rely on the corrupt to get by. I was left to repeat regain consciousness. A trend from that dead end, had come and gone. Left to remain silent just to give the corrupt a chance to return for one more feast; at the end of that lease.

It was handing me the rope and recognition to release

that beast. A need to tie up those loose ends and create a new feast to that beast. It had me interacting with an interface. Effacing another feast, to that entrance that had me regaining conscious awareness again.

I was out for revenge taught a lesson that left me to return for another vision. It had me face another trace enter the edge of reason and follow up on another abrasion. For that occasion, had come and gone, it left me humble, warned me of what was to come from that outcome.

For the trace had me face a case, it was forcing me to repeat. Heaving at me every time I was presented with a challenge. It had me face a trace at the end of the race. I was broken beyond repair at the corrupts expense. The trend became apparent; I fell into revision; handing me repetition.

For the curse had me rehearse, just so I can return and reverse. It had interfaced; it took me in and faced me with final win. For what I assumed was part of the trend ended in tragedy. I had to start again, a new lead that had me reprieve. It took me in and faced me with a test I could not detest.

For I assumed I had my free ride, because I was the chosen one. In fact, I was chosen; not the way I thought. I was to clear the corrupts debts taken for a ride hit with a down fall and left to repeat so never see light. I hit a final deception to that redemption, given a reason to hit back with treason.

It was part of a trace, that had me face another case. It

gave me a trend that broke the silence and had me start again. Not only I was on the mend but the journey had me start again. It gave me a trace that had me replace a case. it forced me to redo and follow up on another clue.

I was given a reason to face a trace, a treason to catch up and face a final case. A proposition that handed me a position. The way it was given handed me a trap in-between that forced me to return and break the silence in the end of that division handing me a brand-new competition.

For the thought took over and the interest; it took a turn for the worst. It gave me a chance to return and curse that verse. It shook my energy and drained me first. It was way off, and I was accepting a defeat had followed up on a trace. A last resort that led me to believe the debt was reprieved.

I was to achieve my goal with repetition, handing the corrupt a final competition. In the end, I got to live my life no longer pretending the trace was pending. Because pretending had me hit a dead end. There was no faith, the trace was cut short and I was handed the last resort.

I assumed everyone I met took me in and handed me another debt; to that death threat. As if it was part of a trace that had me on the edge, it was repeating a brand-new thread; that left to imagination. It caused an effect that had me resign from that delay that handed me denial.

It had me face a redemption to that manifestation. A

journey that took me in broke, the silence and gave me a chance to hit back in advance. I was taught a valuable lesson. I was left to the interrogate the corrupt at every destination. My patience tested, warning me of the energy that served me.

I was left to erase, give in and finalise that energy from within. It forced me to gamble a scheme in-between that theme. I had to get in and accomplish another win, forced to repeat rebel against the corrupts spell. It took me in on a pathway of recovery, establishing a key that brought me forward.

I had to rebuild and step into a challenge that had me surrender. It was handing the corrupt an energy that forced me to repeat. It had me get in and win another inning. I would have been there earlier if I was given the right opportunity but I was used abused let down and in the end.

I had to let go revealing a no show. Returning for one more yearning, creating a trace that will fill in the gaps. Handing the corrupt a dead end in the end of that trend. It had me surrender and follow up on a showcase like no other. It had me presenting the corrupt with a challenge that stirred me up.

It caused an effect, forced me to reset and start fresh. Because those who knew had served me well, it had me race to the end warning me the only troubles that come my way was the energy that had me press replay. It had reached that limit on the condition I lose my soul; on an impure momentum.

It was purely for me to lose my dignity. Apparently the corrupt knew me well. What they knew was part of whom I was at that moment. In the end I had to entrap, then adapt; feeding off the trauma. Handing it back to the corrupt threefold. It was the only way I could resurrect, align; pay out a debt.

The corrupt were returning for a yearning. It was part of a chance to hit back in advance. Facing me every time I was handed a challenge. It that had me embrace another trend at the end of that dead-end. So, when the time come, I could overcome rebuild and regain conscious awareness again.

It had me face with a trace that was on the rise ready to enlarge and hand me surprise. It was part of a well-established momentum. It handing me a chance, to coherent in advance. I was given a reason to embrace and entrance, entrap, and face on a case at the end of that trend; while I start again.

I was causing effects; it had me break the silence. All while I face a condition, that taught me a lesson. It added to my proposal it gave me a second chance to hit an ending that was pending. A drama that was never ending. It had me face a trace; a conviction to that mission.

It led me astray, handing me energy every step of the way. It took me back in time and gave me a chance to repair a damage; that had left me scarred. So, when I reach my peak the only drama left was the one that handed me a clue and gave me a moment to skip that trend right through.

It led me astray; it gave me a chance to belt the corrupt in advance. It broke the silence in the end having me step forward hurdling the one thing that served me well and presented me with an upcoming spell. I had to break the silence end of that repetition and hand the corrupt a dead end.

No competition, no friendly reminder, just a failed redemption; to that repetition. It took me in and handed me revision; I was served a presentation at every proposal. I had my free trial a challenge that had me hit back with a trend, just to get back on track and feed of that trend that startled me

That proposal, ended in my favour, I was given a chance to clear the debt. It had me forced to hit back with remorse. Where the only thing left, gave me a chance to hit back in advance. I was causing effects handing the corrupt a dead ends at the end of that trend.

Giving me the permission and the interpretation that every journey was creating the wrong manifestation. I was to hit back with treason. Creating a challenge to help me rise above and beyond. For what it was worth the drama took over an I was stuck facing another tremor.

It had me on the run, warned of what was to come. For that dilemma, took me on a pathway that had me reap a reward. I was facing on expense that wanted me to wait and awake from that hate that made me believe I was loved. In fact, I was trapped in a trend, that had me face a dead end.

The earlier I rose from that loss the more I competed. It was handing me the loyalty card. I had to remain vigilant to the game and dream an impossible dream. Just to make sure when I reach of shore no one can make it happen unless they attempt to end their life and resurrect.

Then attempt to take a plunge and reason with me. Where now I am way to unbelievably untrustworthy. For the game had me on the edge, ready to replay and finalise another tremble at the end of that simplicity that served me well. It had me face another trace at the end of the race.

I was heading for a fall, trapped in the middle of a case. It had me fast forward at the end of the race. It was part of a game with the same impossible train of thought. It gave me a sense of relief knowing the corrupt had no leeway at the end of that trend breaking the silence.

I was led towards a case that had me on the edge ready to repeat and replace. For the journey ended with an impossible task it gave me a chance to repeat delete delay and follow up on a journey that had me press replay. I was given a chance to hit back in advance.

Warning me I was on the edge, of repeating a new improved meeting. It was given me the impression I hit the end of that return. It had me creating the opposite effect, handing me a delay every time I press replay. Just to follow up on a journey that had me release that beast.

To get to where I am; was a given. Kindly tell me, from where I was, how the hell did I get in so quick. Was it because, I left, lured me back in. Returning the favour so they can get back on track. I parting ways, with the corrupt, handed them a chance to make my light unbright; belting me at every bite.

It was part of a hunt down that led me towards a countdown. It gave me a chance to witness; I was being held hostage. By those who wanted to hit me run a use me as an eyewitness in the long run. It was part of a conceded concession. It took over my vision and turned me into an oblivion idiot.

It was time I gave in returned the favour and force the corrupt to lose everything. A rude awakening a challenge that led me to believe I was not in nowhere near I was meant to be. Because I was not there yet I was working on my craft to make it happened. The corrupt on the other end desiring it.

Time to pretend

ABOUT THE AUTHOR

Panagiota Makaronis

I am not going to boast about myself, my education my family values or views. In the end what can I say life is what it is and everyone has their presentation.

What level of education I have is not important here, the fact that I have lived through death threats, dead ends, and the Demons in my head is enough for me to say! Good reddens, to hard labour.

Life to me has been nothing but expectations with several disappointments, on the hope I get somewhere trusting people when they were meant to help me was another story.

Having said that how many times have I heard people say I am helping you, I let my guard down and it ends up a never-ending Drama a story. Where if I was to repeat will end up worse than the first.

Every goal I set for myself so far though, I have achieved. This book is one of them.

But at what expense I had to endure, just so I do not lose faith in myself and in Humanity along the way. Others who knew could not wait to trace test my patience on the hope they erase my passion and end the race before me.

Because I was living and breathing in a society full of competitors, trying to compete with me and entering my realm on the hope they can harm me for they assumed that had more man power than me.

My theory is just to prove that the world is Governed, not just by everyone you meet but also by the way you witness and see yourself. It plays a huge part when you are about to end one journey and rehearse a new path.

A journey I wish not to return and replay, if anything I just want to move forward not look back and return for revenge. Because my opponent lost a fight and could not harm me so he decided to alarm everyone on the hope they cave in on it start an Allianz and harm me that way.

It left cursing the ones who were reversing and rehearsing, just so they can return stir the pot and leave me stagnant. Stuck in a world of my own sitting in self-pity, no way out unless I fought my way out.

That created more war in my peace because those who knew me, knew me well, fighting back was the only way they can prevent going through hell.

In the end all it did, was make things worse, for they were making mountains out of mole hills. However, the interpretation was enough for me to see I was on the right track the risks I took was based on not losing my faith or myself because others were doubting me and create anomaly.

They were haunted by me and my spirit they could not handle my presence or wait to see where they could hit me and run with a dead-end challenge. The only way out was to hold on to my dream repeat rebel and hit with an All might Spell.

I had come across several individuals who could not wait to break my fighting spirit, constantly on the move of how to kill me and my spirit.

The constant rejection, let down from those stalkers who had nothing better to do then follow me everywhere. Enter my realm just before I am about to make it happen, it got to the point I was failing every test because of it.

Eventually I gave in it was evident, let my Guard down on the hope and the condition there abuse and their method return and back fires.

Having to pick myself up after being pushed straight of the edge from so called Evil! Family friends and Associates, those who I call the corrupt.

What can I say a job is a job well done, level of education is based on life lessons? Everyone has a theory and so do I. Whether you agree is another story to just agree to disagree.

All the studying I did gave me an outlook, a method and outcome where sometimes I look back and wish I never entered but again I would not be here if I didn't.

The theory of here see and speak no evil to me is a lesson lived and lesson learnt. A challenge I can honestly say, it was testing a trace for me to embrace look back and erase. As I face my fears overcome another failure to that feast that handed me release.

As I look ahead and watch my journey unfold with a story untold, it will become a final phase to the next part of my truth. A challenge that will give me the indication I was on my path a feast to release peace.

Everyone is looking for answers and the hope to live

through life with comfort passion and a reason without having to deal with treason.

My memoirs are based on my journey and life lessons, it is all in the book in the end only time will tell, what can I say will be me, keeping up with the programme my way.

Not the way they state it because I hesitate to wonder who is really saving me here. For in the end the matter of facts, is in my hands, because I am an individual. My thoughts are based on my life lessons and no one can challenge or change that.

I know every challenge has its presentation and what I see is I am about to shut one door and open another. Where my vision is no longer impaired and whatever is enlisted to get to this point is no longer in the back burner.

It belongs in my spirit it is mine I earned it! I am just messenger, just passing through the rest remains Ancient History added with a Mystery.

For those who read will understand read between the lines, because my point of view is a venture to next quest on hope I can make a difference to humanity for the next generation to read and interpret my vision as a composition not a competition!

Happy Reading!

THE THEATRICAL MELODIA OF MY LIFE: CHRONICLE ONE

This book is based on my journey, the roller coaster I call life, my thought patterns, and my experiences. How I overcome so many turmoils, how I changed my perception, for it led me towards a destination that gave me tension.

The Throne Of Ruby An Endless Emerald Affair: Chronicle 26

The Throne of Ruby an endless Emerald Affair of Glory, Chronicle 26; a challenge I could not resist. It gave me power; an energy to persist. Not only I could see, the reality to that treaty, kick in.

Burning Crown Of Glory: Chronicle 25

Burning Crown of Glory; Chronicle 25. The continuation of my Memoirs.
I found myself in a position of questioning the motives of certain individuals. I was put in a situation, that

had me forced to override, run hide, and return when needed. The clock was ticking, and those who were relentless and ruthless were scheming.

A Sinful Act Of Kindness From The Heart : Chronicle 24

A Sinful Act of Kindness from the Heart; Chronicle 24. A continuation to my memoir; The Theatrical Melodia of my Life. Where one day at a time took a wrong turn, a least expected accident turned my life upside down. An unexpected nightmare. Exiting my comfort zone and hit with another dead end.

A Byway Chariot Awaits An Awakening Contingency: Chronicle 23

A Byway Chariot Awaits, an Awakening Contingency; Chronicle 23. A continuation of The Theatrical Melodia of my Life; Chronicle 1. My Epistemology Theory, an Odyssey; My Bible! I swear by it! Where I fell into a trap and a trace that became part of a worrisome outcome.

The Iconic Door To Peace My Souls Final Feast A True Awakening: Chronicle 22

The Iconic Door to Peace, my Souls Final Feast, A true Awakening; Chronicle 22. A technicality to rectify a task from the past arose. It was to bring forth peace, torn at every trace an insightful memory; I was to replace a line up, for a belting. For what the corrupt did, just to speed up the process; was priceless.

www.ingramcontent.com/pod-product-compliance
Lightning Source LLC
Chambersburg PA
CBHW032051150426
43194CB00006B/492